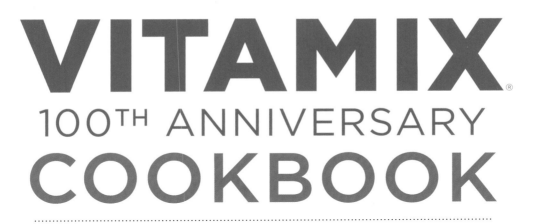

VITAMIX®
100TH ANNIVERSARY
COOKBOOK

100 WHOLE FOOD RECIPES FROM OUR FANS & FAMILY

JODI BERG, PhD
PRESIDENT & CEO OF VITAMIX

Vita-Mix® Corporation | Cleveland | 2021

Jodi Berg, PhD, is the fourth-generation President and CEO of Vitamix,®
a 100-year-young, family-owned developer and manufacturer of
high-performance blending equipment. As she says: "When my great-
grandfather started the company, one of his objectives was to help
people understand the power of whole foods. That's still the heart of
what we do. It's why I'm so passionate about ensuring that every choice
we make, every process we institute, and every product we create helps
us achieve our mission: to create relationships for life by designing,
developing and producing the world's best performing and most reliable
blending solutions."

All the information in this book is not intended to treat, cure, or prevent any disease and should not be considered a substitute for professional medical advice, diagnosis, or treatment. The reader assumes full responsibility for consulting a qualified healthcare professional regarding health conditions or concerns, and before starting a new diet or health program.

Vitamix is not responsible for any adverse reactions, effects, or consequences resulting from the use of any recipes or suggestions in this book.

Nutritional Disclaimer: All the information in the *Vitamix 100th Anniversary Cookbook* is intended for informational and educational purposes only, and has not been evaluated by the Food and Drug Administration. The nutritional information for recipes in this book is provided as a courtesy and is an estimate only.

Vitamix has no responsibility for the persistence or accuracy of URLs for external or third-party Internet Websites referred to in this publication and does not guarantee that any content on such Websites is, or will remain, accurate or appropriate.

Cover and interior design by Aespire® {aespire.com}. Recipe food photography by Tad Ware & Company {tadware.com}. Printed in USA by AGS Custom Graphics, an RR Donnelly Company.

31 30 29 28 27 26 25 24 23 22 21   1 2 3 4 5

ISBN-13: 978-1-7357457-0-1

Library of Congress Cataloging-in-Publication Data has been applied for.

To all the amazing people—employees, beloved fans, health advocates, superusers, home chefs, foodservice professionals, family, and friends— who have helped Vitamix give the gift of health for 100 years! Thank you for being part of our big, beautiful, multigenerational, global Vitamix family!

FOR BONUS CONTENT & MORE RECIPES

Look for the QR codes throughout the book and scan with your mobile device to explore more content on Vitamix.com.

Check out our online library of whole food blending recipes! Visit **100.Vitamix. com/recipes**

CONTENTS

Foreword.. 1

A Passion for Health for 100 Years 2

The Vitamix Legacy 18

Why Whole Foods?... 22

Techniques & Tips 28

Smoothies 34

Beverages 52

Dips & Spreads 66

Dressings 82

Sauces & Sides... 92

Soups.. 110

Quick Breads & Cookies 126

Desserts & Treats 136

Baby Foods.. 158

Pet Treats 166

Vitamix Essentials 174

Recipe Index.. 178

Gratitude 184

FOREWORD

Before I read the *Vitamix 100th Anniversary Cookbook*, I expected it to have a place of honor on the bookshelves of The Chef's Garden and The Culinary Vegetable Institute. That's because I know Jodi Berg. I know Vitamix. I know their commitment to whole foods, to quality, and to providing the world's best health-related products.

I got to know Jodi as she generously gave of her time and talents at our annual Food & Wine and, most recently, our Roots conferences, where culinary leaders from all around the globe gather on our grounds to discuss their work with like-minded individuals who share a passion, commitment, and motivation to improve our food system.

Jodi's family was actually way ahead of the curve, thanks to the vision of her great-grandfather, William Grover Barnard Sr., and her grandparents, Bill and Ruth. During times when they faced financial challenges, they took an unwavering stand for whole food health. They understood the value of a plant-based diet and its role in wellness.

Their philosophy resonates deeply with me and with my farming family. My father, Bob Jones Sr., would encourage us to be as good as the farmers were 100 years ago—in other words, to be as savvy and forward thinking as Jodi's great-grandfather.

Every morning when my brother Bob and I get up before the sun rises, we are fully committed to doing whatever we can to regeneratively farm the most nutritious and delicious vegetables possible, providing farm-fresh ingredients that people can use in their Vitamix, inspired by this cookbook's recipes.

During our 2017 Roots conference, Jodi shared how her mother told her she could accomplish anything she wanted—and the *Vitamix 100th Anniversary Cookbook* proves the truth of that statement.

Well done, Jodi! Well done.

Farmer Lee Jones
The Chef's Garden and The Culinary Vegetable Institute

COMMITTED TO WHOLE FOODS

The Chef's Garden aims to grow and ship the highest quality and most nutritious and flavorful vegetables and herbs, while maintaining a commitment to ecologically friendly and sustainable agricultural practices. Visit **Farmer JonesFarm.com**

A PASSION FOR HEALTH FOR 100 YEARS

Meet the generations behind our anniversary celebration.

Vitamix—the company my great-grandfather started, still 100% family owned, a brand that is beloved by people all around the world, and a multigenerational family that includes employees, suppliers, vendors, customers, and communities—is celebrating its 100th year "young" anniversary. I say young because even though we have made a difference in the lives of millions of people, we are just getting started. There is still a large percentage of people who have yet to discover the power of whole food and high-performance kitchen equipment.

A centennial company can't be created in a single lifetime, but it can be celebrated on behalf of all the generations of amazing people who have built the platform upon which we get to bring forth the Vitamix purpose of "liberating and nourishing the zest for life."

This book is a mere sampling of the creativity and passion of our founder; of my grandparents, father, aunts, and uncles; of the thousands of employees, some across multiple generations, that have worked for us over the past 100 years; and of our millions of beloved fans and multiple communities in which our employees and facilities are located.

Ownership extends through several family branches, reaching into the sixth generation, as represented by some at a Vitamix gathering.

I recognized more than 10 years ago that it would take an army to change the way the world thinks about food. We are a battalion in that army and we—the global Vitamix family—are changing the lives of generations to come through the understanding and enjoyment of whole food.

OUR FAMILY'S PASSION, 100 YEARS STRONG

Vitamix's 100th anniversary has given me quite the opportunity to look back at the history of this company. The stories of the Vitamix family—which includes my ancestors and relatives; our employees and their families; our suppliers and vendors; and our customers and communities—have intertwined to create a powerful legacy. And that legacy is this: the knowledge that whole foods bring incredible joy and health to our lives.

This alone brings me unbelievable delight. But as my great-grandfather, William Grover Barnard Sr. (whom everyone affectionately calls "Papa") would have said, "But wait, there's more."

Not only has Vitamix become iconic in the eyes of our fans and followers, but it has become resilient across generations and through crises. And the reason for both is our purpose-driven culture.

Being iconic, resilient, and purposeful did not happen overnight, or solely because of things that have occurred in my lifetime. Similar to how a pearl is the result of an oyster turning a negative into a beautiful jewel, Vitamix grew to the gem that it is by navigating crises, embracing opportunities, focusing our passion on our purpose, and never, ever giving up. So that you can truly appreciate the people behind the stories and recipes in this book, allow me to share a few nuggets of the history we have created—together.

As each generation of the Barnard family—I'm the fifth family CEO and a member of the fourth generation—has come into leadership positions at Vitamix, they've brought unique strengths that were exactly what the company needed at the time to release and empower the creativity, innovation, and passion of the greater Vitamix family.

If you are a member of our extended Vitamix family, you know this already. Passion is one attribute that we all share. We are passionate about a lot of things—the first being to make the world a better place.

That passion has transcended 100 years and began with my great-grandfather. Papa Barnard was passionate about people, life itself, and our duty to serve. You can probably already see how these qualities built a

OUR GUIDING PRINCIPLES

We passionately believe:

✓ In making the world **a better place**

✓ Every person **matters** and can make a difference

✓ Our future depends on **learning** and **innovation**

✓ In embracing our **past** while creating our **future**

✓ In treating people with **dignity** and **respect**

c.1950

foundation for health and joy through whole foods, resilience, and purpose, but let me start with how it drove the pillar of perseverance that our company still stands for today down into our cultural bedrock.

PERSEVERE: UNWAVERING COMMITMENT TO SUCCEED

In the early 1900s, Papa had been successful enough to volunteer all his time serving his community. He was a mayor, undertaker, and railroad station agent among other things, with a young wife and two sons. His world came crashing down when he lost his beloved bride to the Spanish flu; then a steep economic decline, a precursor to the Great Depression, took everything he had worked hard to achieve. He was at a crossroads. He knew he needed to do something different to support his young family, and giving up was not an option. The concept of perseverance, never giving up, has been a part of our company DNA ever since.

Papa Barnard, my great-grandfather, was passionate about everything, but especially whole food health. His enthusiasm came through in promotions for the first Vitamix.

"Thank you, Papa, for making perseverance a foundation for our company and for carrying on through the Great Depression, the hard life of traveling from town to town, and moving your business to Cleveland, because it was the right thing to do."

The Natural Foods Institute in downtown Cleveland was the precursor to today's Vitamix.

Our employees have always been the heart of our company. So much so that my ancestors relocated our company to Cleveland in 1938 after discovering a work ethic and passion in the people of northeast Ohio that mirrored their own. (We have since found this wonderful work ethic in other communities around the world.) Together with his son William Grover Barnard Jr. (my Grandpa Bill), along with Bill's wife (my Grandma Ruth), Papa opened a health food store in downtown. Eventually my grandparents put down stakes just outside of Cleveland, in Olmsted Township, where they raised their family in the little log house Grandpa built by hand, and grew their company with first-generation employees (some of whom have grandchildren working with us still today).

The Vitamix offices eventually grew up next to this small home filled with love and hard work. It stands today at the entrance of our headquarters, a lasting reminder of Grandpa Bill's big dreams and the value of perseverance.

Papa taught his family well. He, Bill, and Ruth navigated momentous changes to life brought about by World War II. They worked in lockstep with suppliers to source materials that were not critical to the war effort, kept people employed, traveled the U.S. teaching people how to eat healthy with the rations they were given, and raised a family—all while growing this company and contributing to their community, as Papa and Grandpa were not able to enlist directly.

My Grandpa Bill built this wooden home himself; a later version stands on Vitamix company grounds.

"Thank you, Grandpa, for passing the torch of perseverance to your children. They never gave up, either, for which so many of us will forever be grateful."

Each of Bill and Ruth's six children were a part of Vitamix over the years and persevered in their own ways. Noteworthy was their oldest son, Grover ("Grove") who put his dream of earning a master's degree in statistics on hold for more than 30 years to stand with his parents so their passion for health and whole food could be supported by his passion for data and quality.

c.1953

c.1970s

In the 1960s, the company was above water but struggling as the U.S. was becoming more and more enamored with processed foods. Grove made great personal sacrifices, even foregoing a paycheck and living with his family in the Vitamix offices for a while. Together my grandparents and their son Grove faced another crossroads.

Ruth and Bill (back, third and second from right) stand with their children John, Virginia, and Grover (back) and Patricia, Frank, and Bonnee (front). Bill poses with an Action Dome lid.

"Thank you, Grandpa, Grandma, and Uncle Grove, for choosing to take a path that had never been traveled before, one that again set our course for becoming who we are today."

During the 1965 World's Fair in New York, the Vitamix pavilion showcased whole food blending.

They went against cultural trends and persevered with their passion, knowing that it would take effort to change the way the public thought about what they ate. They focused the company on enabling people to benefit from whole foods—not just by creating high-performance products, but by walking alongside them and helping them in their whole foods journey. That approach continues to spark joy in all of us who work at Vitamix as well as creating a bond with all who join the Vitamix family.

If we are going to focus on *whole food* nutrition, we need to do it better than anyone else. WILLIAM GROVER BARNARD JR.

Grandpa was passionate about whole food health and Grove was passionate about quality and performance. Together, with the help of employees and customers, they envisioned a machine that was more versatile, more powerful, more efficient, and more effective than a blender. The Vitamix was no longer just a blender and would continue to transform the industry from that moment forward. They did not do it alone. My Grandma and the growing Vitamix family were changing the way people thought about food, one person at a time.

c.1960s

In her tiny home kitchen, Grandma Ruth developed many techniques and recipes for using the Vitamix to create delicious whole food dishes.

My Grandma was working quietly behind the scenes in the kitchen of that little log cabin, putting the Vitamix through its paces. Grandma and Grandpa ate a vegetarian diet—at a time when that was anything but mainstream! She was like a mighty one-woman product development department: She came up with various techniques that would spark ideas for product enhancements. It was Grandma who discovered that you can make hot soup with fresh vegetables in the Vitamix, thanks to the friction its action generated in the container.

I remember my Grandma's laughing eyes and joy in living; she lifted up and supported her husband as he juggled the many balls he always threw into the air. Only after she was on her own did we find out how strong and smart and a force to be reckoned with she was. Her influence threads through all the recipe books and product literature we've published over the years ... and even weaves into this very book, where you'll find some of Grandma's historic recipes.

> When someone refers to the *Vitamix family*, they could mean the people that work at Vitamix or the family who started the company. In a lot of ways they are one and the same.
>
> RUTH BARNARD

Grandma inspired customers, and employees and customers inspired her, resulting in techniques and recipes only possible in the Vitamix—like grinding grain, chopping, creating whole grain muffins, smoothies, frozen desserts, hot soup, sauces and dressings. One of my own

Vitamix employee Lynn Pace was a familiar face in advertising and recipe books as she showcased the Vitamix's capabilities.

family's favorite is homemade Raw Applesauce spread over Whole Wheat Bread—all prepared in the Vitamix! (You'll find those recipes on pages 95 and 129.)

Grove's brother John—my father—persevered like all his siblings, traveling with his parents to fairs and shows, demonstrating, packing boxes and opening mail and all the tasks that come with being a kid in a family that owned a business. He went to college and earned an engineering degree, married, and moved away. During his multiple-decade sabbatical from the family business, he resolutely pursued other ventures and raised a family of his own. Dad did eventually come back, joining the Vitamix engineering department and filing more than 70 U.S. and international patents for new features and functions.

I like to describe my Dad as being "planted deep"—solid and unwavering, a man of integrity and humility. He treated people with respect and led by example, making him a wonderful CEO. Upon his return to the company he introduced the Flurry, the first commercial Vitamix machine for the foodservice market, still making frozen mix-in treats around the world. He and his brother Frank then developed the Vitamix equipment that's indispensable to smoothie shops, coffee shops, and restaurants, consistently creating many millions of drinks, smoothies, sauces, soups, and sorbets in more than 130 countries. They made it look easy, but I remember the conversations around

the dinner table as they leapfrogged technology to create a machine that could withstand the impact of rock-solid ingredients, process small or large amounts equally well, and be durable without compromising on reliability or performance. This technology was brought into our household units and is still part of the magic behind most of the models we sell today.

"Thank you, Dad and Uncle Frank, for never giving up and persevering against the odds. Your ingenuity and authentic inclusion of talented employees, suppliers, and customers transformed the foodservice industry in ways that equally transformed lives."

Standing on the shoulders of the giants that came before, I have had the distinct pleasure and honor of persevering through incredible growth, as our customers began shouting the benefits of whole food and the need to have a Vitamix through the megaphone that social media was creating.

Communities crossed borders, transcended language barriers, and spread the message of whole food health around the globe. The Vitamix family was unified in a way that was never possible before. Our fans professed their love for our products and we professed our commitment to them to never compromise on quality and performance. People have been sharing their ideas, recipes, and techniques with us, and we have been listening, learning from their creativity, and creating what we call the WOW! We are persevering into a whole new realm as we head into the next century.

Before he discovered the Vitamix, Papa Barnard sold the Polly Can Opener beginning in 1921. It helped people safely open cans of healthy produce.

"A big thank you to all or our employees, their families, their communities, our fabulous followers, and fans. It is YOU who persevere to change the lives of people forever."

VITALITY: COMMITMENT TO HEALTHY LIVING

Just as perseverance is a core tenet of our company, so is our dedication to helping people vitalize their lives with whole food. Back in 1921, Papa Barnard could have chosen to sell anything, but he focused on a product that would allow people to eat produce all year round: a can opener. Now, it sounds crazy to think that a can opener could help people eat healthier. In the years after World War I, canned goods were coming onto the consumer market, but people were using sharp knives to open them. The Polly Can Opener allowed families to eat healthy canned fruits and vegetables without mom or dad hurting themselves opening the cans.

More than an appliance for making drinks, the very first Vitamix helped consumers extract maximum nutrition from whole fruits and vegetables.

Papa had an innate ability to communicate that message of value and healthy living to people as he began traveling around and demonstrating this revolutionary product. He was intuitive and empathetic; he told the story of this product as a solution to a problem in a way that was so relevant, and the Barnard Sales Company took hold.

These days, we understand more and more about the connection between what we eat and how we feel. But back in the 1920s, '30s, and '40s that was a pretty revolutionary concept. No one had heard the phrase, "You are what you eat." Yet Papa, Grandpa, and Grandma knew deep down that a whole food diet could lead to health and wellness. They experienced it in their own lives. My grandma's father suffered from intestinal issues, and they were delighted (albeit not surprised) that changes in his diet made all the difference. As Papa saw that the country was shifting toward processed food, he tailored more and more of his message to educating folks about why food could impact their well-being. There were a few other notable people at the time who embraced natural foods, many of whom are credited in our archives for working together to spread the message, but most have come and gone. Vitamix is one of the few early adopters of whole food health that continues to this day.

Shortly after Papa changed the company's name to the Natural Foods Institute, he, Grandpa, and Grandma found our headliner product: a blender. At the time, other salesmen were pitching blenders as a way to mix drinks, but Papa knew that it could help people create more wholesome dishes with fresh fruits and vegetables than any of the tools he had sold so far. This first product was truly a blender—that is, until Grandpa and his sons invented the first and only true whole food machine I mentioned earlier: the Vitamix.

With *health*, we have wealth.

WILLIAM GROVER "PAPA" BARNARD

Grandpa followed in his father's footsteps and they took their message from town to town, an exhausting way of life but an effective way to spread the health message. Then Grandpa landed on a big idea, one that made a huge difference for the small company. They were hungry to share their message of good eating and good health with more and more customers, so Grandpa suggested they produce a new thing: a television spot that would come to be known as an "infomercial." Papa wasn't convinced, but Grandpa persuaded his dad to give his product demonstration live on TV in 1949. This half-hour demonstration was so successful they later recorded another one so that Papa and his message of whole food health would be preserved. (You can find it at 100.vitamix.com/infomercial.)

Papa Barnard spread the word about the power of the Vitamix and the benefits of whole foods via a 30-minute TV infomercial.

Under Grove's leadership, the Vita-Mixer 4000 was released.

Papa was in his element, passionate and energetic. He opened the spot by talking directly to viewers about the most vital thing that concerns them: their health. Papa, Grandpa, and Grandma knew then what health experts and our passionate Vitamix fans know today: that blending whole ingredients in the Vitamix delivers all those naturally occurring vitamins, minerals, and nutrients to vitalize our bodies—in the most delicious way possible.

> **We want to make the** *world's best* **health-related products and have the world's happiest and healthiest employees.** WILLIAM GROVER "GROVE" BARNARD, III

Grove's statistical mind turned out to be a critical ingredient to yet another method to improve people's health. During his tenure as president and CEO, Vitamix became legendary in the direct response world with catalogs, newsletters, and mailers that took our whole foods message right to consumers' mailboxes.

When Grove retired, his younger brother John (my father) took the reins. Dad is a true whole foods believer. He may have come by it naturally because he grew up in a vegetarian household, but he is also a convert. The first thing he did when he married my mom and left home was to eat what was socially acceptable. After weight gain and poor health, he came back to a plant-based diet. Now, at the age of 80, he can hike circles around people half his age and he weighs half as much. And I'll tell you: He is truly devoted to his daily green juice; he makes it by the gallon to have on hand all week. In fact, you'll find his Green Smoothie recipe on page 44. Everyone around him sees his vitality and unflagging energy.

Throughout his time as CEO, he'd eat in the Vitamix lunchroom, bringing his own brown bag and sitting down with groups of employees, offering to share an apple or a handful of veggies and good conversation—always exploring new ideas and concepts with whomever was sitting at the table with him.

> **Together, we've succeeded by being honest even if it costs us more, paying for our mistakes, *being loyal* to our customers, and building a product that we know is good for people.**
>
> JOHN BARNARD

2017

c. 2007

c. 2007

My dad is an engineer who understands how to bridge technology, product development, and customer needs.

Here, I hold the Vitamix container upside down to show that the treat I've just blended is frozen to perfection.

Today, the Vitamix is sold in more than 130 countries around the world. We've changed the lives of millions of people. We, the extended Vitamix family, continue to carry the torch of health through whole foods that Papa Barnard lit 100 years ago. And every time we pass that light to others, we inspire them to live their best lives.

"Thank you to the entire Vitamix family worldwide for believing so deeply in liberating and nourishing a zest for life."

PURPOSE-DRIVEN CULTURE

I started out by declaring that we, the entire Vitamix family, are full of passion. Mix passion with a good dose of purpose and you have an iconic centennial story filled with resilience, innovation, and transformation that continues to change lives.

The Barnard family and our extended Vitamix family have been committed to healthy living for 100 years. Our purpose is so personal to us. Before smoothies were hugely popular, before there was a store called Whole Foods,™ before plant-based eating was commonplace, Vitamix embraced these concepts and taught others how to live them. Papa knew that how good we feel is directly connected to what we eat. His son, daughter-in-law, and their children and grandchildren have carried his torch forward not because it was his, but because it is part of who we are. Millions of people globally have lit their torches as well, spreading our message, spreading the gift of health, spreading an uncompromising commitment to quality and performance, spreading our passion and purpose.

While we share this book to honor our 100th anniversary, that's not its sole reason for being. Really, it's a celebration of the larger Vitamix family—our employees and, most important, our customers all around the world. This collection of recipes includes some of my Grandma's "greatest hits" alongside favorites from Vitamix fans that will inspire you to use your Vitamix in all kinds of exciting new ways.

You are a member of our Vitamix family and part of the next chapter of the story that we're just beginning to write. We welcome you on this journey to vitality, and we're grateful for your support and friendship. **Enjoy!**

> "We know that how long people live and how good they feel is directly related to the *choices they make* about what they eat and how they live their life. By educating people about this reality and providing them a tool to make the healthier food choices easy and delicious, lives have been changed. JODI BERG

THE VITAMIX LEGACY

Discover our 100-year history of nourishing the zest for life.

1921–1929

William Grover "Papa" Barnard launches a new business selling household products; the Polly Can Opener is an early success.

1939

The family opens a health food store in Cleveland and begins advertising the Vitamix.

1949

Papa Barnard demonstrates the Vitamix on live TV—sparking hundreds of orders—and a new marketing platform, the infomercial, is born.

1937

The Barnard family forms The Natural Foods Institute.

1942

Bill Barnard purchases property in Olmsted Township, outside of Cleveland, and builds a house for his young family; six years later, the business would locate there, too.

Ruth Barnard authors the first book of 500 recipes to make with the Vitamix.

1955
Papa Barnard retires; Bill and his wife, Ruth, assume leadership. Over the years, the family would travel across the country to demonstrate the Vitamix and the health benefits of whole foods.

1962
Bill and Ruth's oldest son, Grover, known as "Grove," returns to the family business.

1966
The company is renamed Vita-Mix Corporation.

1969
Doubling down on its commitment to quality and performance, the company introduces the Vitamix 3600, which is versatile and powerful enough to grind grain, make hot soup, and produce ice cream.

1981
Bill and Ruth's son John joins Vitamix as lead engineer.

1985
Grove (above) becomes Vitamix President, establishes quality standards, and pioneers a direct mail program. The first commercial product, the Flurry, is developed by brothers John and Frank Barnard.

1992
Vitamix introduces the Drink Machine for foodservice use. The Total Nutrition Center, a revolutionary product for home use, debuts.

Vita-Mix

1997
Bill and Ruth's granddaughter, Jodi Berg (above, second from right), joins the company and establishes an international sales and marketing division.

1999
Upon Grove's retirement, John Barnard (above right) becomes President.

2002

Vitamix begins demonstrating products in retail chains, including Costco.

2007

The Vitamix 5200 represents another leap in technology for home blending.

2010

Jodi becomes President and CEO as John becomes Executive Chairman. Vitamix introduces The Quiet One® for commercial use. The Vitamix is featured on QVC for the first time and sets a sales record.

2011

Vitamix celebrates its 90th anniversary.

2012

Popular cooking shows, including *Top Chef®* and *Iron Chef® America* feature the Vitamix.

2009

John Barnard is named CEO and Jodi Berg, his daughter, assumes the role of President.

Vitamix introduces the Professional Series 750 and 7500 models—the next generation in high-performance blending.

2013

Vitamix establishes the Vitamix Foundation to collaborate with other institutions and further the knowledge, consumption, and enjoyment of plant-based whole foods.

Vitamix® FOUNDATION

2014

Vitamix named Best in Class Beverage Blender for one of nine consecutive years by *Foodservice Equipment & Supplies*.

2015

The Vitamix Cookbook: 250 Delicious Whole Food Recipes to Make in Your Blender by Jodi Berg is published with Harper-Collins.

2020

Multiple product introductions include a 48-ounce stainless steel container, a 12-cup Food Processor Attachment, and an Immersion Blender that works in any container.

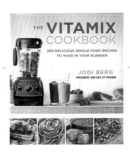

2018

New products include the Personal Cup Adapter, allowing customers to instantly transform their full-size Vitamix into a personal blender, and the Aer™ disc container, a versatile container for whipping, muddling, foaming, emulsifying, and more.

2021

Vitamix celebrates its 100th year as a family-owned business.

2019

Vitamix introduces Vitamix Rewards to celebrate its customers' loyalty and zest for life by encouraging members to engage with the brand in unique ways.

2016

The Ascent® Series launches, with inter-changeable SELF-DETECT® containers.

WHY WHOLE FOODS?

Embrace delicious, nutrient-packed, unprocessed foods.

Our family has steadfastly celebrated the connection between whole food and health for nearly 100 years. If you have been part of our extended Vitamix family for a while now, the concept likely is not new to you. (In fact, some of this information about whole food health was first published in *The Vitamix Cookbook* in 2015.) And the medical science supporting that connection has only strengthened over the years.

As Papa Barnard declared in the first Vitamix infomercial back in 1949: "With health, we have wealth! With our health, we're the richest person on Earth!" He went on to show us how, by using the Vitamix to blend the amazing flavors and nutrients of whole ingredients, we can consume more healthy foods—peels, seeds, skin, and all. He showed us how we can improve our diets and our health without sacrificing flavor or convenience. Papa may have been more of a salesperson than a scientist, but over the years, the research in favor of whole food has stacked up.

However one defines wealth, there is no question that good health has tremendous value. We spend a lot of money on health care annually. A 2019 study funded by the National Heart, Lung, and Blood Institute found that diseases related to diet, such as heart disease, stroke, and Type 2 diabetes, represent $50 billion in U.S. health care costs each year. That's a hefty price tag for our poor eating habits!

But how do we get people eating a better diet? Here at Vitamix, we strongly believe that whole foods are key.

WHAT ARE WHOLE FOODS?

There is a lot of talk about whole foods, and for good reason. In 2014 in the *Annual Review of Public Health*, Dr. David Katz and Dr. Stephanie Meller from Yale University published a study comparing different popular diets. As *The Atlantic*, reporting on their work, concluded:

Papa Barnard shared his own whole food health journey through this monthly newsletter.

"A diet of minimally processed food close to nature, predominantly plants, is decisively associated with health promotion and disease prevention. Nutritionally complete, plant-based diets are supported by a wide array of favorable health outcomes, including fewer cancers and less heart disease. These diets ideally include not just fruits and vegetables, but whole grains, nuts, and seeds as well."

We can, it appears, make a positive impact on our health by eating more whole foods. Papa would not be surprised.

Before we talk about why we should eat more whole foods and how, let me clarify what we here at Vitamix believe they are. To us, whole foods are **foods in or very close to their natural state**, complete with most or all of their nutrients, fiber, phytochemicals, minerals, and the like. Fresh or frozen fruits and vegetables, nuts, seeds, and legumes are all whole foods. Whole grains—unprocessed whole grains such as oat groats, whole wheat kernels, and brown rice—are also whole foods. You get the idea.

Besides just plain tasting good—especially locally grown and organic options—whole foods generally have higher nutrient density. What is nutrient density? It simply means that the foods have a large percentage of nutrients relative to the total number of calories. Blueberries and leafy greens, for example, are considered "superfoods" because have a very large number of nutrients relative to their calories. Nuts, whole grains, legumes, and cruciferous vegetables are, likewise, packed with vitamins, minerals, antioxidants, and phytonutrients that may work to reduce inflammation and prevent disease. Not all whole foods are low in calories of course, but even foods like avocados and nuts are much more nutrient-dense than an equal serving of a more processed snack—even if you eat the same number of calories. Great taste and good nutrition together? Absolutely!

Whole foods are clearly very good for us, but do we eat enough of them? Sadly the answer is still no, and we can't really say it is for lack of awareness about the health benefits of not only fruits and vegetables but all kinds of whole foods. This information was fairly common knowledge even back in Grandpa and Grandma's day, although it was often ignored as people chose foods for convenience.

Research from the Centers for Disease Control and Prevention in 2017 showed that only 10 percent of American adults met the recommended intake of fruits or vegetables each day. The consumption of whole grains and legumes is even less and they are both key to providing the fiber our bodies need. Think about this.

We need to do better—as Papa Barnard would tell us, our health depends upon it! We logically know we should eat more whole food, yet we don't. How can this be?

THE PERILS OF PROCESSED FOODS

Let's talk about processed food. If American adults are eating too few fruits and vegetables, we are arguably eating too many processed foods. According to the American Institute for Cancer Research in 2017, nearly 60 percent of the calories in the food American consumers buy comes from overly processed food, which also tends to have more fat, sugar, and salt content than other foods.

What counts as processed food? The Academy of Nutrition and Dietetics identifies a range. First, there are minimally processed foods like bagged greens. Next they identify foods processed at their peak to preserve nutrition, such as frozen vegetables. Then foods with ingredients—such as sweeteners, fats, or preservatives—added for flavor and texture. Finally, the last category of processed foods includes items like packaged baking mixes or bottled sauces and ready-to-eat foods like crackers and frozen meals.

Fast foods include candy, cookies, breakfast cereals, bars, white flour baked goods, and all other high-calorie, low-nutrient foods that people often eat multiple times per day. They are calorically dense, highly flavored, and nutritionally barren. DR. JOEL FUHRMAN

Just as all whole foods are not created equal, not all processed foods are created equal either, nutritionally speaking. Cut and bagged vegetables or greens (which are technically processed) can make vegetables more convenient to use, although slightly more expensive. Just be sure to check the labels. Some cut and bagged vegetables have additives that enhance flavor or preserve shelf life, so steer clear of those if your desire is for the least-processed whole foods.

The more a food is processed and refined, the more likely it is to lose its naturally occurring fiber, minerals, vitamins, and so forth. But it's not just

that processed food has less nutrition and fiber; it has *more* fat, sugar, and sodium, which themselves lead to poor health. A report from the National Institutes of Health puts it like this:

"In their analysis of the eating habits of nearly 44,000 adults over 16 years, NIH-funded researchers attributed much of our nation's poor dietary showing to its ongoing love affair with heavily processed fast foods ..."

The researchers also identified several key problems in the way most people eat:

- Refined grains, starchy vegetables, and added sugars still account for 42 percent of the average American's daily calories.
- Whole grains and fruits provide just 9 percent of daily calories.
- Saturated fat consumption remains above 10 percent of daily calories, as many Americans continue to eat more red and processed meat.

THE HEALTH BENEFITS OF WHOLE FOODS

The health benefits of whole foods are vast. Because whole foods tend to have higher nutrient density, you can often eat more of them while taking in fewer calories overall, which in turn support maintaining a healthy ideal weight. Fresh fruits, vegetables, grains, and legumes contain fiber, so you are likely to feel fuller for longer, an added advantage.

Cooking and eating whole foods can also be important if you are on a restricted diet. When you prepare whole foods at home, you know exactly what is going into your food. If you put spinach, grapes, banana, berries, and ice in the Vitamix for a smoothie, you will simply get a delicious drink, with no hidden ingredients, preservatives, or other such "surprises."

By preparing foods at home, you can also control the amounts of salt and sugar added to your food. There may very well be a health benefit to the peace of mind that comes with knowing exactly what you are putting into your body, but the scientists have not discovered this yet!

We know that whole foods are important to good health, so the question becomes not why should we eat a more whole-foods-focused diet, *but how?*

If flavor and convenience are important, we here at Vitamix have great news. As this cookbook will show you, healthy cooking can be both simple *and* delicious.

BETTER NUTRITION MADE SIMPLE

When Papa Barnard encountered the blender, he was thrilled. This was the way to bring even more whole foods into people's diets! He was clearly on to something. And as my grandma, Ruth Barnard, realized in 1937, a sustainable whole foods diet needs to taste good and have variety:

"I am gradually assembling more and more tempting dishes, so it is getting easier. Why, I was actually complimented enthusiastically on some of my dishes by the young couple who visited us!"

To meet the demands of our busy lives, we believe it's important that food be simple and quick to prepare. You may not want to sit down to a big bowl of leafy greens first thing in the morning, but drop those greens in a Vitamix with fresh fruit, whip up a delicious smoothie, and suddenly you have a nutritious and delicious breakfast on the go. Combining leafy greens with fruit brings out the sweetness in the greens, allowing the flavors to blend right in. A bit of cooked squash or sweet potato and/or a few legumes can make a smoothie extra smooth! That's a lot of nutrient dense foods first

thing in the morning, making for a powerful way to prepare your body for anything that fills your day! A smoothie makes a delicious breakfast for kids, too; they'll never guess you're sneaking in all those fruits and veggies.

There are lots of ways that you can incorporate whole foods into your diet, but it is quite a challenge to eat the volume of whole food and get the nutrition your body needs without a Vitamix. The Vitamix allow you to use the whole food so you retain all its innate nutrients. The sweet pineapple core is too fibrous to chew but can be blended up into a juice, smoothie, or sauce. You can purée a whole tomato—skin, seeds, and all—and make a soup or hearty marinara sauce. You can't chew up an orange seed or a flax seed very easily, but a Vitamix can pulverize them almost instantly, where other blenders may struggle with these tougher ingredients.

> **One of the most powerful steps you can take to improve your health is to incorporate more *plant-based recipes* into your diet. With my Vitamix, I'm able to make delicious plant-based recipes that are packed with flavor and nutrition and are easy to make!** TAMARA DEGRASSE

Smoothies are a great place to start, but they aren't the only easy way to add more whole foods to your diet. Our classic Vegetable Soup recipe (page 113), for example, contains more than a pound and a half of vegetables. This book is chock-full of delicious recipes that consist of nothing more than fresh fruits and vegetables.

Here at Vitamix, we have a dedicated culinary team that develops all kinds of nutritious and delicious dishes, from smoothies to desserts. Even more, we're constantly inspired by the many Vitamix fans all over the world who find creative ways to marry whole ingredients and global flavors into incredible recipes.

To celebrate our 100th anniversary, we've gathered 100 recipes here—recipes that range from my dad's daily green drink, to my grandmother's homemade applesauce, to our fans' family favorites like "hidden veggies" frozen yogurt. We're excited to introduce you to an array of international dishes, too, like Middle Eastern dips, Italian sauces, and Asian dressings. We hope this book encourages you to enjoy whole foods the Vitamix way: with ease, with pleasure, and with good health.

As Papa says, "Delicious!"

TECHNIQUES & TIPS

Make everyday kitchen tasks easy with your powerful, versatile Vitamix.

TECHNIQUES

The Vitamix is so much more than a blender! Read on to learn how to chop ingredients, grind grain, create hot soups and frozen treats, and more.

Blending

Your Vitamix can handle just about anything you throw in the container. Placing heavier, frozen items on top of lighter ingredients helps weigh them down and gets the blend moving faster. This can also help prevent the blend from stalling. Add ingredients in this order:

1. Liquids (water, juice, yogurt)
2. Dry goods (grains, seasonings, powders)
3. Leafy greens
4. Fruits and veggies
5. Ice and frozen ingredients

For most recipes, you'll get the best results by starting the Vitamix on its lowest speed and quickly increasing to the highest speed. When using a Vitamix with Programs, simply choose the program setting (such as Smoothie or Hot Soup) that's appropriate for the recipe. There are a few exceptions, so always follow the recipe instructions.

For thicker blends, use the tamper as needed to press ingredients toward the blades to produce the ideal flow through the container.

Your Vitamix is powerful enough to pulverize a full container of ingredients. Then, when they start to blend down, you can add even more through the lid plug opening while the Vitamix is running.

WANT MORE TIPS & TRICKS?

Visit **100.Vitamix. com/tips**

Chopping

With a few quick bursts of power, your Vitamix easily rough chops ingredients to create chunky dips, soups, and sauces—no need to use a knife. Make the Vitamix your ultimate kitchen assistant to handle ingredient preparation: Chop carrots and onions, mince garlic, and finely chop fresh herbs for all kinds of recipes. You can also chop nuts and grate hard cheeses with just a couple of pulses. Prepare a big batch of chopped vegetables or grated Parmesan and freeze for future use.

Drop Chopping

Drop ingredients through the lid plug opening while the blades are moving:

- Ice
- Carrots
- Onion
- Garlic
- Peppers
- Hard cheese

Wet Chopping

Break veggies into chunks, place in container and add water to cover; pulse to desired texture, then drain:

- Cauliflower
- Broccoli
- Potatoes
- Fresh herbs

Grinding

With the smooth turn of a dial, transform roasted nuts into homemade nut butter and whole grains into flour or meal. You can also grind rice to create your own gluten-free baking blend. Baked goods are healthier and taste so much better when they're made with freshly milled flour (and it's a budget-friendly option, too). Coarser-grind wheat makes a wholesome hot cereal for breakfast cooked with water, Cashew Milk (page 64), or milk. **See the Vitamix Essentials section beginning on page 174 for recipes including Whole Wheat Flour and Cornmeal and different types of nut butters.** Use this guide to estimate the yield on ground grains:

Whole Kernel Wheat Measurement	Grinding Time	Speed	Approximate Flour Yield	Degree of Fineness
¾ cup (144 g)	1 minute	VAR–HIGH	1 cup + 2½ teaspoons (126 g)	Very fine
1 cup (192 g)	1 minute	VAR–HIGH	1½ cups (180 g)	Very fine
1¼ cups (240 g)	1 minute	VAR–HIGH	1¾ cups + 2 Tablespoons (225 g)	Very fine
1½ cups (288 g)	1 minute	VAR–HIGH	2⅓ cups + 1 Tablespoon (288 g)	Very fine
1¾ cups (336 g)	1 minute	VAR–HIGH	2½ cups + 3 Tablespoons (322 g)	Very fine
2 cups (384 g)	1 minute	VAR–HIGH	3¼ cups (390 g)	Very fine

Puréeing

Nothing purées like a Vitamix; that's why chefs love our products for creating impossibly smooth soups and sauces. Simply blend whole-food ingredients with a bit of water, broth, or cooking liquid to silky perfection.
• Silky purée = 90 seconds
• Chunky-smooth blend = 45 seconds
• Chunky blend = 30 seconds

Whole Food Juicing

Unlike ordinary juicing machines that extract liquid but leave the nutrient-packed solids behind, the Vitamix is powerful enough to transform whole fruits and vegetables into pure, smooth juices. Using your Vitamix for juicing retains all those healthy vitamins, minerals, and antioxidants naturally occurring in skins and pulp. Why throw all the good stuff away? See the sections on Beverages (starting on page 52) and Smoothies (page 34) for whole food recipes.

LOOKING FOR AN UPGRADE OR AN ACCESSORY?

Visit **100.Vitamix. com/shop**

Heating

The friction of the blades can make steaming-hot soup in under 10 minutes, right in the container;* chilled soups take even less time. Create a simple hot soup with fresh vegetables of your choice and a splash of vegetable broth—if you'd like, pulse any add-ins like cooked noodles, rice, or pasta, or fresh herbs after blending. See the Soups category starting on page 110 for a delicious batch of easy soup recipes.

*When blending hot liquids or ingredients in the Vitamix container, use caution, as spray or steam may cause burns. Do not fill container to maximum capacity. Always begin processing on the lowest speed setting, variable speed 1. Keep hands and exposed skin away from lid opening to prevent possible burns.

Emulsifying

Store-bought salad dressings often include artificial flavors and preservatives; it's so much healthier and more delicious to make your own. (Less expensive, too.) It's easy to make homemade vinaigrettes in your Vitamix, because the powerful action creates a perfect blend of oil and other liquids that won't separate after sitting. See the Dressings section including an oil-free version on page 85 for fantastic recipes, or create your own vinaigrette using your favorite flavors following this basic formula:

3 Parts Healthy Oil + 1 Part Acid + Aromatics

Healthy Oils	Acids	Aromatics
• Extra-virgin olive	• Citrus zest	• Garlic
• Grapeseed	• Citrus juice (zest the rind; peel, then use the "meat" of the fruit)	• Onion
• Avocado		• Fresh ginger
• Nut		• Celery
	• Cider or wine vinegar	• Carrot
	• Fruit vinegar	• Shallots
	• Mustard	• Fresh herbs

TIPS FOR PREPARATION

Batters

With the turn of a dial, you can quickly and easily mix batters for pancakes, waffles, cakes, cookies, muffins, and quick breads. No need to take out a mixing bowl, electric mixer, and other kitchen tools; your Vitamix makes breakfast pancakes and after-school zucchini bread so easy to make! A few additional tips:

Fold in Extras
After blending, transfer the batter to a bowl and fold in ingredients like berries, chopped fruit, or nuts.

Very Versatile
The Vitamix is capable of blending not just thin pancake batter, but also heavier doughs for cookies and yeast breads.

Whole Ingredients
Make treats guilt-free by using whole grain flours and natural sweeteners in your baked goods.

Frozen Desserts

Your Vitamix will quickly and easily create frozen desserts, from ice cream and sherbet to fruit sorbet and milkshakes. There's nothing more flavorful than a sorbet made from frozen fruit (especially strawberries or peaches, in season) blended with yogurt and a touch of natural sweetener. Here's what you need to know to make perfect frozen desserts:

The Right Ratios: Containers to Ingredients
- 64-ounce Low Profile: 1½ cup liquid to 1½ pounds frozen ingredients
- 64-ounce Classic/48 ounce: 1 cup liquid to 1 pound frozen ingredients
- 32-ounce: ¾ cup liquid to ¾ pound frozen ingredients

The Right Temperature
Set frozen fruits out at room temperature for about 10 minutes while you gather other ingredients. Softening the frozen fruit just slightly will help create a silky texture in your finished dessert.

VITAMIX REWARDS

Join the program that earns you rewards for each purchase and connects you to online tutorials and activities. Visit **100.Vitamix. com/rewards**

Watch and Listen

After starting the Vitamix, use the tamper to press ingredients toward the blades; this creates an optimal flow in the container. In about 30–60 seconds, the sound of the motor will change and four mounds should form in the mixture. Stop the Vitamix. Do not overblend, or the mixture will melt.

Smoothies/Beverages

A morning smoothie may be the very first thing you made in your new Vitamix when you brought it home—and you're not alone! The sky's the limit when it comes to combining fresh fruits and vegetables (peels, stems, seeds, and all) to create your own personal smoothie recipes. Use these tips and ideas to get you started:

ICE & FROZEN

FRUITS & VEGGIES

LEAFY GREENS

DRY GOODS

LIQUIDS

32 **48** **64**

Load the Container

Mix & Match Ingredients

Choose 1 Liquid:

1 cup soy milk	1 cup fruit juice
1 cup yogurt	1 cup water

Choose 2 Fruits and Vegetables:

1 apple	1 carrot
1 cup strawberries	1 cup peaches
1 cup blueberries	1 cup mango, peeled
1 cup grapes	½ cup papaya, peeled
1 orange, peeled	1 pear
1 cup melon, peeled	2 stalks celery
1 cup pineapple	1 kiwi, peeled
1 banana, peeled	½ cup cucumber

Choose 1 Green: (optional)

2 cups spinach	1 romaine heart
1 cup kale	¾ cup raw broccoli
½ head romaine	1 small head Bibb or Boston lettuce

Before Smoothies Were "In"

Way back in 1949, Papa Barnard blended up a smoothie in his famous TV infomercial.

A Smoother Smoothie

Your Vitamix has all the power you need to transform whole vegetables and fruits into a perfectly smooth beverage. If your smoothie is really thick or frozen, use the tamper to create the ideal flow over the blades.

Make It a Juice!

To transform a smoothie into a juice, place a nut milk bag (or cheesecloth) over a large bowl and carefully pour the mixture into the bag. Squeeze all the liquid out of the pulp into the bowl. The fiber that is left is loaded with nutrients, so consider using it in other recipes.

Super Easy

If using a Vitamix with program settings, place ingredients in the container as noted on page 33 and select the Smoothie setting. Your Vitamix does all the work!

Power Your Days

Use the 64-ounce container to prepare larger batches of smoothies and juices that you can enjoy for several days. Refrigerate in an airtight container for a few days or freeze the extra and put it in the fridge the night before. Just give it a shake before serving.

SMOOTHIES

Papa Barnard knew that when it comes to healthy living, how good we feel (in more ways than one) is directly connected to what we eat. Smoothies have become the most preferred way to incorporate healthy foods into our daily routine—and Vitamix put the *smooth* in smoothie! I remember seeing an old Vitamix ad that featured a "Green Elixir"—I can't say for sure, but this may have been one of the very first green smoothies.

These bright blended drinks are trendy on social media for good reason—they are delicious and *sooo* easy to make. They are also essential to eating healthy and part of everyday life for generations of Vitamix fans.

I'm still inspired by my father, John Barnard, who drinks more smoothies than anybody I know except possibly my mom (see his recipe on page 44). Like my parents, Vitamix fans know that a smoothie is a healthy, enjoyable way to jump start the morning or grab a meal on the go. And because kids love them, blending up a smoothie is an easy way to boost their intake of fruits and veggies. Quite a few years back, a mom told me her 2-year-old would never drink a green smoothie. We filled his sippy cup—and he would not let his mom take it out of his hands. You see, a green smoothie is actually quite sweet because fruit brings out the natural sweetness in most greens.

> " **Green smoothies include greens for** *nutrients and health* **and fruit for sweetness, nutrients, and fiber. With our Vitamix, I make full containers so that my wife and I always have some ready to drink in the refrigerator.** JOHN BARNARD

And unlike other machines that extract juice but leave the nutrient-rich pulp behind, your Vitamix transforms every bit of your whole fruits and vegetables into a super-drink packed with fiber, vitamins, and plant-based protein. When you enjoy a smoothie, you raise a glass with the global Vitamix family and share a commitment to healthy living that's lasted for 100 years.

I hope you're as inspired by these recipes as I am. Blend your favorite, then experiment with other ingredient combinations you and your family love. Check out page 33 for a quick guide to building the perfect smoothie. And make it a great day!

Papa Barnard and his son Bill demonstrated the Vitamix at fairs; this recipe comes from a cookbook sold during those shows.

VITA MIXER

Shared by: Vitamix / *Published in:* 1951 / 64 / 3 servings / *Total time:* 15 minutes

INGREDIENTS

1 lemon

2¼ cups (540 ml) water

1½ medium apple (300 g), halved and seeded

1½ medium bananas (165 g), peeled

3 Tablespoons (25 g) whole raw cashews

1½ small carrots (90 g)

6 leaves romaine lettuce (30 g)

¾ cup (25 g) fresh spinach

1½ Tablespoons raisins

3 sprigs flat-leaf parsley

1½ cups (195 g) ice cubes

INSTRUCTIONS

Use a microplane or grater to zest the lemon. With a peeler or paring knife, remove the bitter white pith (optional). Add the zest and fruit to the container. Place all remaining ingredients into the container in the order listed and secure the lid. Start the Vitamix on its lowest speed, then quickly increase to its highest speed, using the tamper to press ingredients toward the blades. Blend for 45 seconds or until desired consistency is reached.

Amount per (492 g) serving: Calories 190, Protein 3 g, Total Fat 4 g, Carbohydrates 41 g, Cholesterol 19 mg, Fiber 6 g, Saturated Fat 1 g, Sodium 40 mg, Sugar 24 g

Dahlia's Green Smoothie

DAHLIA'S GREEN SMOOTHIE

Shared by: Heidi Barron, Vitamix Fan / **64** / 3 servings / *Total time:* 10 minutes

INGREDIENTS

1 cup (240 ml) non-dairy yogurt or plain yogurt

1 cup (30 g) fresh spinach

1 mango (120 g), pitted and peeled

1 kiwi (60 g)

1 large green apple (230 g), halved and seeded

1 medium banana (120 g), peeled

1 Tablespoon honey or 2 dates, pitted (optional)

2 cups (260 g) ice cubes

INSTRUCTIONS

Place all ingredients into the container in the order listed and secure the lid. Start the Vitamix on its lowest speed, then quickly increase to its highest speed, using the tamper to press ingredients toward the blades. Blend for 45–60 seconds or until desired consistency is reached.

Amount per (420 g) serving: Calories 230, Protein 6 g, Total Fat 2 g, Carbohydrates 50 g, Cholesterol 5 mg, Fiber 5 g, Saturated Fat 1 g, Sodium 65 mg, Sugar 41 g

KALE, BANANA & BERRY SMOOTHIE

Shared by: Diane Mascitelli, Vitamix Fan / **32** **48** **64** / 3 servings / *Total time:* 10 minutes

INGREDIENTS

1 medium banana (120 g), peeled

2 cups (60 g) kale

2 cups (300 g) frozen mixed berries

2 cups (480 ml) **Orange Juice** (see page 176)

INSTRUCTIONS

Place all ingredients into the container in the order listed and secure the lid. Start the Vitamix on its lowest speed, then quickly increase to its highest speed, using the tamper to press ingredients toward the blades. Blend for 45 seconds or until desired consistency is reached.

Amount per (326 g) serving: Calories 170, Protein 3 g, Total Fat 1 g, Carbohydrates 41 g, Cholesterol 5 mg, Fiber 6 g, Saturated Fat 0 g, Sodium 10 mg, Sugar 26 g

> **My Vitamix has allowed me to create** *fond memories* **with my children as we prepare our meals together.** HEIDI BARRON

MORNING WONDER DRINK

Shared by: Terry Echols, Vitamix Fan / **64** / 3 servings / *Total time:* 10 minutes

INGREDIENTS

6 mandarin oranges (445 g), peeled
4 strawberries (165 g)
1 cup (150 g) fresh blueberries
1 ½-inch thick) slice fresh turmeric (5 g)
1 ½-inch thick) slice fresh ginger (4 g)
2 cups (260 g) ice cubes

INSTRUCTIONS

Place all ingredients into the container in the order listed and secure the lid. Start the Vitamix on its lowest speed, then quickly increase to its highest speed, using the tamper to press ingredients toward the blades. Blend for 60 seconds or until desired consistency is reached.

Amount per (343 g) serving: Calories 130, Protein 2 g, Total Fat 1 g, Carbohydrates 32 g, Cholesterol 23 mg, Fiber 5 g, Saturated Fat 0 g, Sodium 5 mg, Sugar 23 g

PAPAYA VANILLA SMOOTHIE

Shared by: Santiago Ortiz, Vitamix Fan / **32** **48** **64** Classic / 1 serving / *Total time:* 10 minutes

INGREDIENTS

¼ cup (40 g) papaya, peeled and seeded
½ small banana (50 g), peeled
1 (½-inch thick) slice pineapple (80 g), peeled
1 cup (30 g) fresh spinach
1 scoop (¼ cup, 20 g) vanilla protein powder, or ¼ cup (30 g) whole raw almonds
1 cup (130 g) ice cubes

INSTRUCTIONS

Place all ingredients into the container in the order listed and secure the lid. Start the Vitamix on its lowest speed, then quickly increase to its highest speed, using the tamper to press ingredients toward the blades. Blend for 45 seconds or until desired consistency is reached.

Amount per (370 g) serving: Calories 120, Protein 3 g, Total Fat 2 g, Carbohydrates 26 g, Cholesterol 16 mg, Fiber 5 g, Saturated Fat 0 g, Sodium 110 mg, Sugar 16 g

"I've been using the Vitamix for the last 10 years. I had to make a change to lose weight and keep off the weight I had lost."
SANTIAGO ORTIZ

Morning Wonder Drink

Spa Smoothie

"As a busy working mom, I really appreciate how *easy* my Vitamix makes everything.

KELLY LEVEQUE

SPA SMOOTHIE

Shared by: Kelly LeVeque, celebrity nutritionist and bestselling author

64 / 3 servings / *Total time:* 10 minutes

INGREDIENTS

1½ cups (360 ml) **Almond Milk** (see page 175)

¼ avocado (40 g), pitted and peeled

1 scoop (¼ cup, 20 g) vanilla protein powder

2 Tablespoons chia seed

Juice of 1 lemon

1 cup (30 g) fresh spinach

1 small Persian cucumber (85 g)

¼ cup (7 g) fresh mint leaves

2 cups (260 g) ice cubes (optional)

INSTRUCTIONS

Place all ingredients into the container in the order listed and secure the lid. Start the Vitamix on its lowest speed, then quickly increase to its highest speed, using the tamper to press ingredients toward the blades. Blend for 60 seconds or until desired consistency is reached.

Amount per (292 g) serving: Calories 110, Protein 7 g, Total Fat 6 g, Carbohydrates 8 g, Cholesterol 15 mg, Fiber 4 g, Saturated Fat 1 g, Sodium 135 mg, Sugar 1 g

PROTEIN SHAKE

Shared by: Debra Brock, Vitamix Fan / **32** **48** **64** Classic / 1 serving / *Total time:* 10 minutes

INGREDIENTS

1 cup (240 ml) **Almond Milk** (see page 175)

1 cup (30 g) organic spinach or kale

½ small organic banana (65 g), peeled

½ scoop (2 Tablespoons, 10 g) protein powder

INSTRUCTIONS

Place all ingredients into the container in the order listed and secure the lid. Start the Vitamix on its lowest speed, then quickly increase to its highest speed, using the tamper to press ingredients toward the blades. Blend for 45 seconds or until desired consistency is reached.

Amount per (371 g) serving: Calories 140, Protein 10 g, Total Fat 4 g, Carbohydrates 19 g, Cholesterol 20 mg, Fiber 2 g, Saturated Fat 0 g, Sodium 250 mg, Sugar 9 g

"I use my Vitamix every morning for the easiest, tastiest, most nutritious shake, and I also make healthy soups. I would never be able to do this with another blender."

DEBRA BROCK

BRIGHT BEET SMOOTHIE

Shared by: Donna Doyen, Vitamix Fan / **48** **64** / 2 servings / *Total time:* 10 minutes

INGREDIENTS

1 small beet (65 g), washed and halved

2 (¾-inch thick) slices pineapple (285 g), peeled and halved

1 medium banana (120 g), peeled

2 Tablespoons flax seed

1 scoop (¼ cup, 20 g) protein powder

1 cup (130 g) ice cubes

INSTRUCTIONS

Place all ingredients into the container in the order listed and secure the lid. Start the Vitamix on its lowest speed, then quickly increase to its highest speed, using the tamper to press ingredients toward the blades. Blend for 45–60 seconds or until desired consistency is reached.

Amount per (323 g) serving: Calories 290, Protein 8 g, Total Fat 15 g, Carbohydrates 35 g, Cholesterol 20 mg, Fiber 2 g, Saturated Fat 2 g, Sodium 65 mg, Sugar 22 g

JOHN BARNARD'S GREEN SMOOTHIE

Shared by: John Barnard, Vitamix Executive Chairman / **64** / 4 servings / *Total time:* 10 minutes

INGREDIENTS

3 cups (165 g) kale or dandelion greens, washed well

¾ cup (180 ml) cold water

1½ cups (226 g) green grapes

½ lime

½ mango (170 g), pitted and peeled

1 medium kiwi (70 g)

⅓ large cucumber (110 g)

1 (2-inch thick) slice fresh ginger (25 g)

1 large carrot (70 g), halved

¼ cup (40 g) flax seed

6 (½-inch thick) slices pineapple (440 g), peeled

1 medium banana (120 g), peeled

1¼ cups (150 g) frozen blueberries

1 cup (130 g) ice cubes

INSTRUCTIONS

Place all ingredients into the container in the order listed and secure the lid; if all ingredients don't fit, start the Vitamix and add remaining ingredients through the lid plug opening while blending. Start the Vitamix on its lowest speed, then quickly increase to its highest speed. Blend for 45–60 seconds, using the tamper to press ingredients toward the blades.

Amount per (455 g) serving: Calories 250, Protein 5 g, Total Fat 4 g, Carbohydrates 54 g, Cholesterol mg, Fiber 8 g, Saturated Fat 1 g, Sodium 30 mg, Sugar 34 g

*Bright Beet
Smoothie*

" Eating *fresh,* healthy
ingredients made in my Vitamix
is a priority for me. DONNA DOYEN

> **The Vitamix gives this smoothie a *smooth, clean consistency,* and it's packed with energizing B vitamins and protein, too.**
>
> DANNY SEO

Mango Turmeric Smoothie

MANGO TURMERIC SMOOTHIE

Shared by: Danny Seo, Editor in Chief, *Naturally Danny Seo*

  64 Classic / 1 serving / *Total time:* 10 minutes

INGREDIENTS

1 mango (155 g), pitted and peeled

1 cup (240 ml) non-dairy yogurt or plain yogurt

¼ cup (15 g) fresh spinach

1 (¼-inch thick) slice fresh turmeric (5 g)

1 cup (130 g) ice cubes

INSTRUCTIONS

Place all ingredients into the container in the order listed and secure the lid. Start the Vitamix on its lowest speed, then quickly increase to its highest speed, using the tamper to press ingredients toward the blades. Blend for 60 seconds or until desired consistency is reached.

Amount per (535 g) serving: Calories 220, Protein 26 g, Total Fat 1 g, Carbohydrates 31 g, Cholesterol 15 mg, Fiber 3 g, Saturated Fat 0 g, Sodium 105 mg, Sugar 28 g

CLASSIC VITAMIX RAINBOW SMOOTHIE

Shared by: Vitamix / *Published in:* 1976 / **64** / 4 servings / *Total time:* 10 minutes

INGREDIENTS

1½ small carrots (115 g)

1 medium orange (130 g), peeled

1 celery stalk (75 g)

½ pineapple (600 g), peeled and chopped

¼ bunch (25 g) flat-leaf parsley

½ medium cucumber (125 g), halved

1 small clove garlic, peeled

½ small banana (50 g), peeled

½ medium apple (100 g), seeded

½ cup (15 g) fresh spinach

¼ cup (5 g) wheat grass

½ small red beet (25 g)

2 leaves romaine lettuce (10 g)

1½ cups (175 g) ice cubes

INSTRUCTIONS

Place all ingredients except ice into the container in the order listed. Start the Vitamix on its lowest speed, then quickly increase to its highest speed, using the tamper to press ingredients toward the blades. Blend for 20 seconds. Remove lid plug and add the ice. Replace lid plug and blend for 1 minute 15 seconds or until desired consistency is reached.

Amount per (364 g) serving: Calories 140, Protein 2 g, Total Fat 1 g, Carbohydrates 34 g, Cholesterol 25 mg, Fiber 4 g, Saturated Fat 0 g, Sodium 50 mg, Sugar 22 g

ORANGE SUNRISE BLENDER DRINK

Shared by: Gina Fontana, Vitamix Fan / / 6 servings / *Total time:* 10 minutes

INGREDIENTS

1½ cups (360 ml) water

2 large oranges (340 g), peeled

2 (½-inch thick) slices pineapple (300 g), peeled

3 large carrots (360 g), halved

¼ teaspoon ground cumin

1 (¼-inch thick) slice fresh ginger (4 g)

7 fresh mint leaves

2 cups (260 g) ice cubes

INSTRUCTIONS

Place all ingredients into the container in the order listed and secure the lid. Start the Vitamix on its lowest speed, then quickly increase to its highest speed, using the tamper to press ingredients toward the blades. Blend for 60 seconds or until desired consistency is reached.

Amount per (310 g) serving: Calories 80, Protein 2 g, Total Fat g, Carbohydrates 20 g, Cholesterol 13 mg, Fiber 3 g, Saturated Fat 0 g, Sodium 55 mg, Sugar 13 g

SEMISWEET GREEN SMOOTHIE

Shared by: Scott Tennant, Vitamix Communications Director

  / 2 servings / *Total time:* 10 minutes

INGREDIENTS

1 cup (240 ml) **Almond Milk** (see page 175)

2 cups (60 g) kale or other greens

1 Gala apple (225 g), seeded

½ medium banana (60 g), peeled

1 cup (130 g) ice cubes

INSTRUCTIONS

Place all ingredients into the container in the order listed and secure the lid. Start the Vitamix on its lowest speed, then quickly increase to its highest speed, using the tamper to press ingredients toward the blades. Blend for 45 seconds or until desired consistency is reached.

Amount per (370 g) serving: Calories 120, Protein 3 g, Total Fat 2 g, Carbohydrates 26 g, Cholesterol 16 mg, Fiber 5 g, Saturated Fat 0 g, Sodium 110 mg, Sugar 16 g

> "This is my daily green smoothie, and it's an important part of my routine. It not only fills me up, it also provides a host of vitamins and minerals."
>
> SCOTT TENNANT

> **Thank you, Vitamix, for helping my family choose *healthier options* and making them easy to make!** GINA FONTANA

Orange Sunrise Blender Drink

mindbodygreen Smoothie

MINDBODYGREEN SMOOTHIE

Shared by: Colleen and Jason Wachob of mindbodygreen

 / 3 servings / *Total time:* 10 minutes

INGREDIENTS

2 cups (480 ml) **Almond Milk** (see page 175)

3 Tablespoons mindbodygreen grass-fed collagen+ powder

1 Tablespoon mindbodygreen organic veggies+ powder

1 medium avocado (140 g), pitted and peeled

1 medium banana (120 g), peeled

2 Tablespoons **Nut Butter** (see page 174) or 2 Tablespoons whole nuts

½ cup (55 g) frozen blackberries

½ cup (55 g) frozen broccoli

INSTRUCTIONS

Place all ingredients into the container in the order listed and secure the lid. Start the Vitamix on its lowest speed, then quickly increase to its highest speed, using the tamper to press ingredients toward the blades. Blend for 60 seconds or until desired consistency is reached.

Amount per (319 g) serving: Calories 260, Protein 10 g, Total Fat 16 g, Carbohydrates 22 g, Cholesterol 11 mg, Fiber 6 g, Saturated Fat 3 g, Sodium 200 mg, Sugar 9 g

SUPER GREEN SMOOTHIE

Shared by: Cindy Molnar, Vitamix Fan / **64** / 2 servings / *Total time:* 10 minutes

INGREDIENTS

1 cup (240 ml) **Almond Milk** (see page 175)

6 baby carrots (70 g)

½ medium green apple (120 g), seeded

1 celery stalk (70 g)

⅓ medium cucumber (100 g)

1 scoop (¼ cup, 20 g) protein powder

1 teaspoon Matcha green tea powder

¼ teaspoon spirulina

1 cup (130 g) frozen pineapple chunks

1 cup (130 g) ice cubes

INSTRUCTIONS

Place all ingredients into the container in the order listed and secure the lid. Start the Vitamix on its lowest speed, then quickly increase to its highest speed, using the tamper to press ingredients toward the blades. Blend for 45 seconds or until desired consistency is reached.

Amount per (326 g) serving: Calories 170, Protein 3 g, Total Fat 1 g, Carbohydrates 41 g, Cholesterol 5 mg, Fiber 6 g, Saturated Fat 0 g, Sodium 10 mg, Sugar 26 g

"Thank you, Vitamix, for helping me live as healthy a life as possible!"
CINDY MOLNAR

What the Pros Use

Baristas and bartenders around the world use a commercial Vitamix to craft coffee drinks and upscale cocktails. You can do the same with your Vitamix at home.

Try the Aer Disc Container

The Vitamix Aer disc container is ideal for unlocking all the natural flavor from citrus and other ingredients while keeping elements of the fruit intact. Find our classic Margarita on the Rocks recipe using the Aer disc container at 100.Vitamix.com/margarita.

Mocktail or Cocktail

Create a nonalcoholic version of any cocktail by replacing the spirit with plain or unsweetened flavored sparkling water.

BEVERAGES

Your Vitamix does so many things well, but it is truly masterful at creating perfectly smooth, refreshing, and delicious beverages: smoothies, juices, coffee drinks, mocktails, and cocktails.

If you enjoy specialty beverages from your favorite local coffee shop or that great craft cocktail spot in your neighborhood, you'll be thrilled to know you can create your favorite specialties right in your home kitchen. Transform whole citrus, seasonal fruits, wholesome nuts, and brewed coffee into sophisticated, fully flavored drinks that can start or end your day and delight your friends and family!

> **A great cocktail should have that** *elevation and concentration* **of purity. That's what we need here: consistency, concentrated elegance, elevation, and purity, and we get it with Vitamix equipment.** WILL HOLLINGSWORTH

Our family's passion for whole food health is enhanced by our passion for quality and performance. With your Vitamix, you can hone your home bartending skills or simply add some fun to your drinks using our revolutionary Aer disc container—its unique perforated blade muddles citrus and other flavorful ingredients to extract maximum flavor, not to mention making a mean cold foam.

Whether you serve your creations with a splash of seltzer water or club soda for a "mocktail" version—or add a spirit to make a traditional cocktail—you're experiencing the same innovation that delights customers in smoothie shops, coffee shops, and restaurants around the world.

My Grandpa and Uncle Grove envisioned a versatile machine that met the needs of the health-conscious home cook. My father and Uncle Frank took it up a BIG notch—to a powerful machine that ignites the passion and talent of social gourmets and professional chefs. The blended drink recipes that we share here come from Vitamix fans all over, including Will Hollingsworth, proprietor of the noted Spotted Owl cocktail bar, who considers the Vitamix one of his behind-the-bar essentials. Let your imagination flow as you use your Vitamix to expand your home drink-making repertoire beyond lattes and margaritas.

CITRUS SANGRIA

Shared by: Vitamix / *Published in:* 1996 / **64** / 8 servings / *Total time:* 10 minutes

INGREDIENTS

2 cups (300 g) green grapes

1 lemon, peeled

1 lime, peeled

¼ grapefruit, peeled

1 slice pineapple (150 g), peeled and halved

24 ounces (720 ml) lemon-lime sparkling water

Pitted dates or honey, to taste (optional)

INSTRUCTIONS

Place all ingredients except sparkling water into the container in the order listed and secure the lid. Start the Vitamix on its lowest speed, then quickly increase to its highest speed. Blend for 1 minute, using the tamper to press ingredients toward the blades.

Pour into a punch bowl or glasses and top with sparkling water.

Amount per (168 g) serving: Calories 40, Protein 1 g, Total Fat 0 g, Carbohydrates 18 g, Cholesterol 17 mg, Fiber 1 g, Saturated Fat 0 g, Sodium 10 mg, Sugar 8 g

From the
Archives
1996

This oldie-but-goodie drink was first published in a recipe book that accompanied the Total Nutrition Center Whole Food Machine.

> **A Vitamix Vita-Prep® 3 remains the most** *indispensable tool* **for extracting elevated, concentrated flavors of fresh ingredients in a craft cocktail bar.** WILL HOLLINGSWORTH

SPOTTED OWL PIÑA COLADA

Shared by: Will Hollingsworth, proprietor/bartender of the Spotted Owl, Cleveland

   / 1 serving / *Total time:* 20 minutes

INGREDIENTS

For the piña colada mix:

1 pint (450 g) coconut sorbet

1 (½-inch thick) slice fresh pineapple, or ½ cup (125 g) pineapple juice

For the cocktail:

1½ ounces (45 ml) piña colada mix

1½ ounces (45 ml) Green Chartreuse or high-proof rum

½ ounce (15 ml) Velvet Falernum or almond syrup

1 cup (130 g) ice cubes

Freshly grated nutmeg, for garnish

INSTRUCTIONS

For the piña colada mix: Place all ingredients into the container in the order listed and secure the lid. If using fresh pineapple, start the Vitamix on its lowest speed, then quickly increase to its highest speed. Blend for 30 seconds. If using pineapple juice, start the Vitamix on its lowest speed, then increase to Variable 5 and blend for 30 seconds.

For the cocktail: Place all ingredients into the container in the order listed and secure the lid. Start the Vitamix on its lowest speed, then increase to Variable 5. Blend for 30 seconds. Serve in a coupe glass with grated nutmeg on top.

Amount per (229 g) serving: Calories 220, Protein 1 g, Total Fat 5 g, Carbohydrates 21 g, Cholesterol 20 mg, Fiber 0 g, Saturated Fat 3 g, Sodium 25 mg, Sugar 20 g

One batch of piña colada mix makes 10–12 cocktails. Store remaining mix in the refrigerator for up to 1 week.

Cachaça is a Brazilian spirit that's most famously used in Caipirinha.

Caipirinha

CAIPIRINHA

Shared by: John Olsen, Vitamix Manager, Territory Sales

48 Aer Disc / 4 servings / *Total time:* 10 minutes

INGREDIENTS

2 limes, ends trimmed and sliced into 4 rounds

8 ounces (240 ml) cachaça

¼ cup (60 ml) honey, or alternative sweetener, to taste

1 cup (130 g) ice cubes

INSTRUCTIONS

Place all ingredients into the Aer disc container in the order listed and secure the lid. Start the Vitamix on its lowest speed, then quickly increase to its highest speed. Blend for 45 seconds. Serve over ice.

Amount per (143 g) serving: Calories 200, Protein 0 g, Total Fat 0 g, Carbohydrates 21 g, Cholesterol 0 mg, Fiber 1 g, Saturated Fat 0 g, Sodium 1 mg, Sugar 18 g

LIME MINT AGUA FRESCA

Shared by: Vitamix / **48** Aer Disc / 4 servings / *Total time:* 10 minutes

INGREDIENTS

2 limes, ends trimmed and sliced into 4 rounds

2 cups (480 ml) water

1 cup (130 g) ice cubes

10 fresh mint leaves

The Aer disc container muddles the ingredients to get maximum flavor out of the whole fruit.

INSTRUCTIONS

Place all ingredients into the Aer disc container in the order listed and secure the lid. Start the Vitamix on its lowest speed, then quickly increase to its highest speed. Blend for 45 seconds. Serve over ice.

Amount per (185 g) serving: Calories 10, Protein 0 g, Total Fat 0 g, Carbohydrates 4 g, Cholesterol 0 mg, Fiber 1 g, Saturated Fat 0 g, Sodium 5 mg, Sugar 1 g

" **Feel like you're relaxing on Copacabana Beach while enjoying the national cocktail of Brazil.** *Uma delícia!* JOHN OLSEN

WHOLE FRUIT CHERRY MARGARITA

Shared by: Vitamix / *Published in:* 2016
64 / 6 servings / *Total time:* 10 minutes

INGREDIENTS

1½ cups (360 ml) cold coconut water

6 ounces (180 ml) tequila

2 ounces (60 ml) triple sec or Grand Marnier

1 medium orange, peeled and halved

1 lemon, peeled

1 lime, peeled

⅓ cup (105 g) **Date Syrup** (see page 176)

1 cup (130 g) frozen pitted dark sweet cherries

5 cups (650 g) ice cubes

INSTRUCTIONS

Place all ingredients into the container in the order listed and secure the lid. Start the Vitamix on its lowest speed, then quickly increase to its highest speed, using the tamper to press ingredients toward the blades. Blend for 55 seconds or until desired consistency is reached.

Amount per (254 g) serving: Calories 190, Protein 1 g, Total Fat 0 g, Carbohydrates 25 g, Cholesterol 0 mg, Fiber 2 g, Saturated Fat 0 g, Sodium 0 mg, Sugar 22 g

"As someone who can't stay out of the kitchen, *I rely on* my Vitamix. I love having a handy kitchen tool like this that can make an incredible, healthy meal in just a few minutes. DR. MARK HYMAN

Ultra-Creamy Cashew Butter Coffee

ULTRA-CREAMY CASHEW BUTTER COFFEE

Shared by: Dr. Mark Hyman, advocate of functional medicine

  64 / 1 serving / *Total time:* 10 minutes

INGREDIENTS

1 cup (240 ml) fresh brewed coffee

2 Tablespoons cashew butter

1 Tablespoon **Coconut Milk** (see page 175)

2 teaspoons hazelnut extract (optional)

Cocoa powder or sea salt, for finishing (optional)

This recipe can easily be scaled to 6 servings in your 64 ounce container.

INSTRUCTIONS

Place all ingredients into the container in the order listed and secure the lid. Start the Vitamix on its lowest speed, then quickly increase to its highest speed. Blend for 45 seconds. Garnish with cocoa powder or sea salt, if desired.

Amount per (295 g) serving: Calories 190, Protein 6 g, Total Fat 14 g, Carbohydrates 10 g, Cholesterol 28 mg, Fiber 1 g, Saturated Fat 4 g, Sodium 5 mg, Sugar 0 g

ICED COFFEE PROTEIN DRINK

Shared by: Liz Enyon, Vitamix Fan / **48** **64** / 2 servings / *Total time:* 10 minutes

INGREDIENTS

1 cup (240 ml) water

¼ cup (60 ml) non-dairy yogurt or vanilla yogurt

2 scoops (½ cup, 40 g) protein powder or vegan protein powder

½ small banana (75 g), peeled

1 cup (30 g) fresh spinach

2 teaspoons instant coffee

¼ cup (33 g) ice cubes (optional)

INSTRUCTIONS

Place all ingredients into the container in the order listed and secure the lid. Start the Vitamix on its lowest speed, then quickly increase to its highest speed, using the tamper to press ingredients toward the blades. Blend for 45 seconds or until desired consistency is reached.

Amount per (479 g) serving: Calories 140, Protein 17 g, Total Fat 2 g, Carbohydrates 16 g, Cholesterol 50 mg, Fiber 1 g, Saturated Fat 1 g, Sodium 125 mg, Sugar 9 g

> "I love how rugged the Vitamix is. I make one or two smoothies a day, and it's still kicking."
> **LIZ ENYON**

> **I have used my Vitamix to** *better the lives* **of my family and friends every day since I got it. Thank you, Vitamix!**
>
> BRENDA CRAWFORD

CASHEW MILK

Shared by: Brenda Crawford, Vitamix Fan

64 / 8 servings / *Total time:* 10 minutes

INGREDIENTS

1 cup (150 g) whole raw cashews

7 cups (1.70 l) cold purified water

1 Tablespoon MCT oil (optional)

Pitted dates or maple syrup, to taste (optional)

Pinch of salt (optional)

INSTRUCTIONS

Place all ingredients into the container in the order listed and secure the lid. Start the Vitamix on its lowest speed, then quickly increase to its highest speed. Blend for 1 minute or until desired consistency is reached. Refrigerate for up to 3 days; shake before serving.

Amount per (229 g) serving: Calories 104, Protein 3 g, Total Fat 8 g, Carbohydrates 6 g, Cholesterol 1 mg, Fiber 1 g, Saturated Fat 0 g, Sodium 2 mg, Sugar 1 g

Keep It Healthy

Using non-dairy milk, tofu, or nuts lends a creamy profile to dips and spreads without added oil. Build flavor using spices and herbs instead of salt.

Make Prep Easy

Use your Vitamix to handle all the work before a gathering: Chop vegetables, mince fresh herbs, and blend beverages.

Customize Texture

Your Vitamix creates dips and spreads in a range of textures, from smooth to chunky. If using a Vitamix with program settings, simply select the Dips/Spreads option.

Sweet Touches

Chocolate-hazelnut spread and freshly ground nut butter make delicious accompaniments to fresh fruit.

Big Batches

Vitamix makes entertaining effortless! The 64-ounce container is the ideal size for blending big batches of dips to feed a crowd.

DIPS & SPREADS

When my grandparents first shifted their diet from processed foods to whole grains, fruits and vegetables, and other plant-based foods, Grandma Ruth became a real advocate. She wrote dozens of letters to friends and relatives, in which she described this new way of eating. Grandma Ruth marveled at the health benefits she and Grandpa Bill experienced. She encouraged family members to increase their intake of whole foods and shared the recipes she was developing. You might wonder how I know this. My Grandma was a prolific writer and she made copies of all her letters using carbon paper—that was before the computer was introduced. (Fun fact: My grandmother was the first person I knew to have a laptop—I didn't even know what a laptop was at the time!)

> **I have two personal Vitamix blenders, two for my business, and I have recommended it for the past 20 years. My students and clients have been purchasing them on my recommendation.** JOANNE GERRARD YOUNG

My Grandma also loved to invite people into her home and prepare healthy and delicious meals that made them smile and ask for seconds. She was always trying new dishes and creating new ways to use the Vitamix. You can do as she did and whip up healthy options like smooth and creamy hummus or chunky tomato salsa when friends and family drop by—they make satisfying snacks alongside fresh veggies or whole-grain crackers for dipping.

You'll notice that the dip and spread recipes in this book represent culinary traditions from around the world. What a great way to introduce friends to the pure essence of whole foods by serving them flavorful dishes like the Northwest African purée called *Matbukha*, a chunky Latin American black bean dip, or a vibrant herb-flecked hummus. With a presence in countries across the globe, the extended Vitamix family is all about celebrating and sharing the pleasures of whole-food health!

Vitamix has a global reach—this cookbook was published for Great Britain. The following pages feature several international recipes.

TOMATO SALSA

Shared by: Vitamix / *Published in:* 2009 / **48** **64** / 8 servings / *Total time:* 10 minutes

INGREDIENTS

3 large tomatoes (420 g), halved

1 medium onion (120 g), peeled and halved

½ jalapeño, seeded

1 Tablespoon red wine vinegar

¼ teaspoon salt (optional)

¼ teaspoon ground black pepper

INSTRUCTIONS

Place all ingredients into the Vitamix container in the order listed and secure the lid.

For a chunky salsa: Select Variable 2. Pulse 5–6 times, using the tamper to press ingredients toward the blades. Pulse until desired consistency is reached.

For a smooth salsa: Start the Vitamix on its lowest speed, then quickly increase to its highest speed, using the tamper to press ingredients toward the blades. Blend for 45 seconds or until desired consistency is reached.

Amount per (71 g) serving: Calories 15, Protein 1 g, Total Fat 0 g, Carbohydrates 3 g, Cholesterol 2 mg, Fiber 1 g, Saturated Fat 0 g, Sodium 5 mg, Sugar 2 g

GREEN GODDESS HUMMUS

Shared by: Lisa Bryan, real food lover and creator of the website and YouTube® channel Downshiftology

  / 12 servings / *Total time:* 10 minutes

INGREDIENTS

2 cans (800 g) chickpeas, drained, reserve liquid

⅓ cup (80 ml) chickpea liquid

½ cup (120 ml) **Tahini** (see page 97)

¼ cup (60 ml) extra-virgin olive oil or additional chickpea liquid

1 cup (30 g) fresh spinach

½ cup (20 g) fresh parsley leaves

2 lemons, peeled, or juice of 2 lemons

1 green onion

1 garlic clove, peeled

1 teaspoon ground cumin

¼ teaspoon salt (optional)

Extra-virgin olive oil, chopped herbs, and chopped walnuts, for garnish (optional)

INSTRUCTIONS

Place all ingredients into the container in the order listed and secure the lid. Start the Vitamix on its lowest speed, then quickly increase to its highest speed, using the tamper to press ingredients toward the blades. Blend for 60 seconds or until desired consistency is reached. Garnish as desired for serving.

Amount per (98 g) serving: Calories 200, Protein 7 g, Total Fat 12 g, Carbohydrates 18 g, Cholesterol 3 mg, Fiber 5 g, Saturated Fat 2 g, Sodium 150 mg, Sugar 3 g

---

HUMMUS

Shared by: Mira Gil, Vitamix Distributor, Israel /   / 16 servings / *Total time:* 10 minutes

INGREDIENTS

2 cups (330 g) cooked or canned chickpeas, liquid reserved

½ cup (120 ml) reserved chickpea liquid

¼ cup (60 ml) extra-virgin olive oil, or chickpea liquid

½ lemon, peeled

1 garlic clove, peeled

½ cup (60 ml) **Tahini** (see page 97) or sesame seeds

Ground cumin to taste

¼ teaspoon salt (optional)

INSTRUCTIONS

Place all ingredients into the container in the order listed and secure the lid. Start the Vitamix on its lowest speed, then quickly increase to its highest speed, using the tamper to press ingredients toward the blades. Blend for 1 minute.

Amount per (41 g) serving: Calories 110, Protein 3 g, Total Fat 8 g, Carbohydrates 7 g, Cholesterol 0 mg, Fiber 2 g, Saturated Fat 1 g, Sodium 45 mg, Sugar 1 g

> **Getting my first Vitamix was a total *game changer* in the trajectory of my wellness journey. I consider it one of the best investments in my health.** LISA BRYAN

Green Goddess Hummus

Matbukha

This flavorful purée originates in Northwest Africa; serve it with toasted whole wheat pita bread or fresh vegetables.

MATBUKHA

Shared by: Chen Assor, Vitamix Distributor, Israel / **64** / 12 servings / *Total time:* 3 hours

INGREDIENTS

½ fresh red chili pepper (15 g)

4 garlic cloves, peeled

5 tomatoes (700 g)

1 medium red bell pepper (200 g), seeded

⅓ cup (80 ml) extra-virgin olive oil (optional)

1 teaspoon paprika

¼ teaspoon salt (optional)

Ground pepper to taste

INSTRUCTIONS

Place chili pepper, garlic, tomatoes, and bell pepper into the container and secure the lid. Start the Vitamix on its lowest speed, then quickly increase to its highest speed, using the tamper to press ingredients toward the blades. Blend for 30 seconds.

Transfer mixture to a saucepan; add olive oil (if using). Bring to a simmer, then reduce heat to low and cook for 3 hours, or until mixture is reduced to about one-quarter the volume. Add paprika, and salt and pepper to taste; cook for 10 minutes more.

Amount per (84 g) serving: Calories 90, Protein 1 g, Total Fat 6 g, Carbohydrates 8 g, Cholesterol 2 mg, Fiber 1 g, Saturated Fat 1 g, Sodium 15 mg, Sugar 6 g

BLACK BEAN DIP

Shared by: Laresa Waller, Vitamix Manager, U.S. Shows Sales / **64** / 3 cups / *Total time:* 10 minutes

INGREDIENTS

2 (14-ounce, 400 g) cans black beans, rinsed and drained

2 limes, peeled

2 Roma tomatoes (200 g)

½ cup (25 g) fresh cilantro leaves

1 jalapeño, seeded

2 teaspoons ground cumin

½ cup (75 g) crumbled feta cheese (optional)

INSTRUCTIONS

Place all ingredients except feta into the Vitamix container in the order listed and secure the lid.

For a chunky dip: Select Variable 2. Pulse 5–6 times, using the tamper to press ingredients toward the blades. Pulse until desired consistency is reached.

For a smooth purée: Start the Vitamix on its lowest speed, then quickly increase to its highest speed, using the tamper to press ingredients toward the blades. Blend for 45 seconds or until desired consistency is reached.

Garnish with crumbled feta for serving.

Amount per (52 g) serving: Calories 40, Protein 2 g, Total Fat 1 g, Carbohydrates 6 g, Cholesterol 0 mg, Fiber 2 g, Saturated Fat 3 g, Sodium 35 mg, Sugar 0 g

> **My friends expect me to bring this irresistible dip to every gathering. Surrounded by fresh, crunchy crudités, this *vibrant dish* looks stunning. Who says party food can't be healthy?** KAREN HICKS

BEET BORANI

Shared by: Karen Hicks, Vitamix Manager, Marketing International

  / 16 servings / *Total time:* 15 minutes

INGREDIENTS

For the borani:

¼ cup (60 ml) non-dairy yogurt or plain Greek yogurt

¼ cup (60 ml) extra-virgin olive oil (optional)

1½ Tablespoons sherry vinegar

4 medium red beets (450 g), roasted

1 garlic clove, peeled

½ teaspoon sea salt (optional)

For the topping:

⅓ cup (50 g) feta cheese

1 Tablespoon extra-virgin olive oil (optional)

Pinch of nigella seeds

Pinch of fennel seeds

Pinch of red pepper flakes

Pinch of caraway seeds

INSTRUCTIONS

For the borani: Place all ingredients into the container in the order listed and secure the lid. Start the Vitamix on its lowest speed, then quickly increase to its highest speed, using the tamper to press ingredients toward the blades. Blend for 30 seconds or until desired consistency is reached.

For the topping: Mix all ingredients in a bowl and refrigerate. Sprinkle over the borani just before serving.

Amount per (20 g) serving: Calories 35, Protein 1 g, Total Fat 3 g, Carbohydrates 2 g, Cholesterol 2 mg, Fiber 1 g, Saturated Fat 1 g, Sodium 20 mg, Sugar 1 g

Borani is an Iranian appetizer served with toasted whole wheat pita bread or fresh vegetables. If using the 64-ounce container, you can double the ingredients.

Vegan
Ricotta
Cheese

VEGAN RICOTTA CHEESE

Shared by: Cameron Szatala, Vitamix Fan /   64 / 16 servings / *Total time:* 10 minutes

INGREDIENTS

2 cups (400 g) firm tofu

3 Tablespoons (20 g) nutritional yeast

2 Tablespoons extra-virgin olive oil

1 Tablespoon **Tahini** (see page 97) or sesame seeds

1 lemon, peeled, or juice of 1 lemon

1 medium shallot (30 g), peeled

2 garlic cloves, peeled

½ cup (10 g) fresh basil leaves

1 Tablespoon fresh oregano leaves

1 teaspoon **Soy Milk** (see page 176), plus more as needed

¼ teaspoon salt (optional)

Ground black pepper to taste

INSTRUCTIONS

Press tofu for 10 minutes to remove excess moisture.

Place all ingredients except soy milk into the container in the order listed and secure the lid. Start the Vitamix on its lowest speed, then quickly increase to Variable 4, using the tamper to press ingredients toward the blades. Remove lid plug and add soy milk through the opening until desired consistency is reached.

Amount per (34 g) serving: Calories 50, Protein 3 g, Total Fat 4 g, Carbohydrates 2 g, Cholesterol 1 mg, Fiber 5 g, Saturated Fat 0 g, Sodium 19 mg, Sugar 3 g

TOFU DIP

Shared by: Norma Gustafson, Vitamix Fan / 64 / 32 servings / *Total time:* 15 minutes

INGREDIENTS

3 pounds (1.35 kg) firm tofu

1 lime, peeled, or juice of 1 lime

½ cup (120 ml) prepared yellow mustard

½ cup (120 ml) water

¼ cup (60 ml) extra-virgin olive oil

¼ cup (60 ml) balsamic vinegar

2 Tablespoons Italian seasoning

2 Tablespoons liquid aminos

2 Tablespoons **Tahini** (see page 97)

2 Tablespoons sesame oil

1 Tablespoon chipotle chili powder

¼ teaspoon salt (optional)

Ground black pepper to taste

INSTRUCTIONS

Place all ingredients into the container in the order listed and secure the lid. Start the Vitamix on its lowest speed, then quickly increase to its highest speed, using the tamper to press ingredients toward the blades. Blend for 1 minute or until desired consistency is reached.

Amount per (119 g) serving: Calories 140, Protein 8 g, Total Fat 10 g, Carbohydrates 5 g, Cholesterol 0 mg, Fiber 0 g, Saturated Fat 2 g, Sodium 230 mg, Sugar 1 g

"I love my Vitamix! We can make meals from scratch in just one day that can take days of preparation."
NORMA GUSTAFSON

PLANT-BASED MOZZARELLA

Shared by: Joanne Gerrard Young, Vitamix Fan / 32 48 / 6 servings / *Total time:* 4 hours

INGREDIENTS

¼ cup (35 g) raw cashews, soaked in water to cover overnight and drained

1 cup (240 ml) water

1 Tablespoon nutritional yeast

3 Tablespoons (23 g) tapioca starch

Pinch of onion powder

Pinch of sea salt (optional) and ground black pepper

INSTRUCTIONS

Place cashews, water, and nutritional yeast into the container and secure the lid. Start the Vitamix on its lowest speed, then quickly increase to its highest speed. Blend for 25 seconds. Reduce speed to Variable 3. Remove lid plug and add the tapioca starch through the lid plug opening. Secure lid plug and blend an additional 5 seconds. Season to taste with onion powder, salt, and pepper.

Transfer mixture to a saucepan and heat over medium-high, whisking constantly, until the mixture is stretchy and begins to pull away from the sides of the pan. Allow to cool, then shape into balls. Store in a sealed container in the refrigerator for up to 5 days.

Amount per (50 g) serving: Calories 50, Protein 2 g, Total Fat 3 g, Carbohydrates 5 g, Cholesterol 0 mg, Fiber 1 g, Saturated Fat 0 g, Sodium 4 mg, Sugar 1 g

ALMOND BUTTER TWIST

Shared by: Eliot Martir, Vitamix Senior Dealer Account Rep

 48 64 / 24 servings / *Total time:* 15 minutes

INGREDIENTS

4 cups (600 g) whole roasted unsalted almonds

¾ cup (180 ml) coconut oil or almond oil (optional)

1 teaspoon ground cinnamon

8 dates (120 g), pitted

INSTRUCTIONS

Place all ingredients into the container in the order listed and secure the lid. Start the Vitamix on its lowest speed, then quickly increase to its highest speed, using the tamper to press ingredients toward the blades. Blend for 2 minutes 30 seconds or until desired consistency is reached.

Amount per (28 g) serving: Calories 170, Protein 4 g, Total Fat 15 g, Carbohydrates 7 g, Cholesterol 0 mg, Fiber 2 g, Saturated Fat 5 g, Sodium 0 mg, Sugar 3 g

> "During my time in Customer Service, I took many calls that made it clear that we have a direct impact on people's lives and the way they eat."
>
> **ELIOT MARTIR**

This plant-based cheese alternative melts beautifully on pizza.

Plant-Based Mozzarella

I swear by the Vitamix in my own kitchen and in all of my cooking classes. I always tell my students that the Vitamix is a *necessary tool* for any kitchen.

JOANNE GERRARD YOUNG

HAZELNUT SPREAD

Shared by: Petra Scott, Vitamix Fan

  32 48 64 / 28 servings / ***Total time:*** 10 minutes

INGREDIENTS

2 cups (300 g) whole roasted unsalted hazelnuts

½ cup (75 g) whole roasted unsalted cashews

2 Tablespoon unsweetened cocoa powder

4 dates, pitted, or ¼ cup (25 g) powdered sugar

3 Tablespoons (25 g) bittersweet dark
chocolate chips

3 Tablespoons (45 ml) coconut oil (optional)

¼ teaspoon sea salt (optional)

INSTRUCTIONS

Place all ingredients into the container in the order
listed and secure the lid. Start the Vitamix on its
lowest speed, then quickly increase to its highest
speed, using the tamper to press ingredients toward
the blades. Blend for about 2 minutes or until smooth.

Amount per (16 g) serving: Calories 100, Protein 2 g,
Total Fat 9 g, Carbohydrates 5 g, Cholesterol 0 mg,
Fiber 1 g, Saturated Fat 2 g, Sodium 0 mg, Sugar 2 g

"

**I can't imagine my life without
a Vitamix. It's hands-down the**
most used **small appliance in
my kitchen.** PETRA SCOTT

Usage Ideas

Homemade dressing is so full of flavor, you'll need less on your salad. You can also use the recipes here to drizzle over cooked vegetables or as a dip for raw ones.

. . . .

Skip the Oil

A blend of vegetables and seasonings, along with a bit of lemon juice or apple cider vinegar, makes a terrific fat-free vinaigrette. If you do use oil, make it a heart-healthy option like olive or avocado.

Storage Tips

Transfer homemade dressing to an airtight container and refrigerate for up to 1 week.

DRESSINGS

I n this era of convenience foods, many families have multiple bottles of store-bought salad dressing lined up on the refrigerator shelf. But I'm here to tell you that if there's one thing you can absolutely be making yourself instead of purchasing, it's salad dressing.

One of the most powerful things you can do to improve your health is to substitute homemade items—salad dressing, pasta sauce, soup, and such—for store-bought. You deserve to control what you put into your body, and as a bonus, homemade dressing is more economical.

> "One important element that makes my Nutritarian dietary recommendations unique is that I stress the importance of eating a raw green salad daily. *Most important* is that the dressing is made from nuts and seeds, not oil. —DR. JOEL FUHRMAN

Dressings of every kind are just so easy to make in the Vitamix. My dad loves a big salad with dinner, and you'll find his Vegetable Dressing recipe on the facing page. He starts with a juicy, ripe tomato and then adds other vegetables he and Mom happen to have on hand: carrots, celery, maybe a bell pepper, and a pinch of pepper.

Everything goes into the container—seeds, peels, and all—creating a purée so vibrant and full of flavor. Use nuts or tofu to create a creamy texture, or go with fruit to add a natural sweetness. Toss it with a bowlful of fresh greens and other flavorful ingredients, and the dressing creates a "super salad" that everyone at the table just loves.

Making your own salad dressing means you know exactly what goes into it. Take a look at the label on a bottled dressing, and you'll find additives like flavoring and preservatives. When you skip the oil and minimize the salt, you can be proud that you created a blend that's healthier than anything you can buy.

VEGETABLE DRESSING

Shared by: Vitamix / *Published in:* 1975 /   32 48 64 / 12 servings / *Total time:* 10 minutes

INGREDIENTS

1 large Roma tomato (140 g)

½ lemon, peeled

1 garlic clove, peeled

1 medium red bell pepper (170 g), halved and seeded

1 celery stalk (60 g), halved

Honey to taste (optional)

Pinch of salt (optional)

Pinch of ground black pepper

INSTRUCTIONS

Place all ingredients into the container in the order listed and secure the lid. Start the Vitamix on its lowest speed, then quickly increase to its highest speed. Blend for 45 seconds or until desired consistency is reached.

Amount per (34 g) serving: Calories 10, Protein 0 g, Total Fat 0 g, Carbohydrates 2 g, Cholesterol 1 mg, Fiber 1 g, Saturated Fat 0 g, Sodium 30 mg, Sugar 1 g

Feel free to use whatever vegetables you have on hand.

From the
Archives
1975

This versatile dressing is a Vitamix classic! The recipe debuted in a 1975 cookbook showcasing the Vitamix blade reversal technology.

VIETNAMESE DRESSING

Shared by: Bobby Berk, interior designer and host of Netflix's *Queer Eye*®

  64 / 24 servings / *Total time:* 10 minutes

INGREDIENTS

1¾ cups (420 ml) **Coconut Milk** (see page 175)

2 limes, peeled, or juice of 4 limes

1 Tablespoon rice vinegar

2 Tablespoons honey

2 Thai red chilies, seeded

2 garlic cloves, peeled

½ cup (20 g) fresh cilantro leaves

1 medium avocado (140 g), halved, pitted, and peeled

INSTRUCTIONS

Place all ingredients into the container in the order listed and secure the lid. Start the Vitamix on its lowest speed, then quickly increase to its highest speed, using the tamper to press ingredients toward the blades. Blend for 30 seconds.

Amount per (28 g) serving: Calories 50, Protein 0 g, Total Fat 5 g, Carbohydrates 3 g, Cholesterol 0 mg, Fiber 1 g, Saturated Fat 3 g, Sodium 1 mg, Sugar 2 g

---

SESAME DRESSING

Shared by: Vitamix / *Published in:* 2015 / 8 servings / *Total time:* 10 minutes

INGREDIENTS

¾ cup (180 ml) soy milk

2½ Tablespoons (35 ml) soy sauce

2½ Tablespoons (35 ml) rice vinegar

1 date, pitted, or 1 teaspoon honey

⅓ cup (50 g) sesame seeds

INSTRUCTIONS

Place all ingredients into the container in the order listed and secure the blade base. Start the Vitamix on its lowest speed, then quickly increase to its highest speed. Blend for 20 seconds.

Amount per (30 g) serving: Calories 40, Protein 2 g, Total Fat 3 g, Carbohydrates 3 g, Cholesterol 0 mg, Fiber 1 g, Saturated Fat 0 g, Sodium 170 mg, Sugar 1 g

Vietnamese Dressing

Dressing

> "A Vitamix is the Nutritarian's best friend, as we make delicious and *super healthful* sauces, dressings, and dips for vegetables. DR. JOEL FUHRMAN

Orange Sesame Dressing

ORANGE SESAME DRESSING

Shared by: Dr. Joel Fuhrman, bestselling author of *Eat for Life* and pioneer of the Nutritarian Diet

  64 / 30 servings / *Total time:* 10 minutes

INGREDIENTS

¼ cup (60 ml) apple cider vinegar

2 large (500 g) oranges, peeled and quartered

¼ cup (30 g) toasted sesame seeds, divided use

¼ cup (30 g) whole raw cashews

1 Tablespoon fresh lemon juice

INSTRUCTIONS

Place the apple cider vinegar, oranges, 2 Tablespoons toasted sesame seeds, cashews, and lemon juice into the container in the order listed and secure the lid. Start the Vitamix on its lowest speed, then quickly increase to its highest speed, using the tamper to press ingredients toward the blades. Blend for 30 seconds or until desired consistency is reached. Top the dressing with the remaining 2 Tablespoons of toasted sesame seeds.

Amount per (22 g) serving: Calories 20, Protein 1 g, Total Fat 1 g, Carbohydrates 3 g, Cholesterol 2 mg, Fiber 1 g, Saturated Fat 0 g, Sodium 0 mg, Sugar 2 g

NUTRITARIAN CAESAR DRESSING

Shared by: Dr. Joel Fuhrman, bestselling author of *Eat for Life* and pioneer of the Nutritarian Diet

   / 16 servings / *Total time:* 10 minutes

INGREDIENTS

½ cup (120 ml) water

½ cup (170 g) silken tofu

¼ cup (60 ml) lemon juice, or 1 lemon, peeled

⅓ cup (45 g) whole raw cashews

¼ cup (30 g) hemp seed

3 garlic cloves, peeled

2 celery stalks (140 g)

4 dates, pitted

2 Tablespoons nutritional yeast

1 Tablespoon Dijon-style mustard

½ teaspoon white miso

½ teaspoon kelp granules

¼ teaspoon ground black pepper

INSTRUCTIONS

Place all ingredients into the container in the order listed and secure the lid. Start the Vitamix on its lowest speed, then quickly increase to its highest speed. Blend for 30 second or until desired consistency is reached.

Amount per (32 g) serving: Calories 35, Protein 2 g, Total Fat 2 g, Carbohydrates 3 g, Cholesterol 1 mg, Fiber 2 g, Saturated Fat 0 g, Sodium 35 mg, Sugar 1 g

RASPBERRY DIJON DRESSING

Shared by: Randall Weiss, Vitamix Demonstrator /   / 22 servings / *Total time:* 10 minutes

INGREDIENTS

½ cup (120 ml) balsamic vinegar

¾ cup (95 g) fresh raspberries

¼ lime, peeled

2 garlic cloves, peeled

2 teaspoons Dijon-style mustard

5 fresh basil leaves

2 dates, pitted, or honey to taste

Pinch of ground white pepper

½ cup (120 ml) avocado oil (optional)

INSTRUCTIONS

Place all ingredients except avocado oil into the container in the order listed and secure the lid. Start the Vitamix on its lowest speed, then quickly increase to its highest speed. Blend for 30 seconds. If using the avocado oil, reduce speed to Variable 3. Remove lid plug and slowly pour oil through the opening. Replace lid plug and blend on highest speed for 10 seconds.

Amount per (18 g) serving: Calories 60, Protein 0 g, Total Fat 5 g, Carbohydrates 2 g, Cholesterol 1 mg, Fiber 0 g, Saturated Fat 1 g, Sodium 10 mg, Sugar 1 g

NON-DAIRY CAESAR DRESSING & SALAD

Shared by: Marilu Henner, actor, author, podcaster, and memory expert

  / 8 servings / *Total time:* 15 minutes

INGREDIENTS

1 large egg yolk

2 garlic cloves, peeled

1 teaspoon Worcestershire sauce

1 teaspoon Dijon-style mustard

1 Tablespoon fresh lemon juice, or ½ lemon, peeled

4 anchovies

⅓ cup (80 ml) olive oil

3 heads romaine lettuce, washed and chopped

¼ cup (60 g) grated soy parmesan

Ground black pepper to taste

INSTRUCTIONS

Place the egg yolk, garlic, Worcestershire, mustard, lemon juice, and anchovies into the container and secure the lid. Start the Vitamix on its lowest speed, then increase to Variable 3. Blend for 30 seconds. Remove lid plug and slowly pour oil through the opening. Replace lid plug and blend on highest speed for an additional 10 seconds.

In a large serving bowl, toss romaine lettuce with dressing; sprinkle with soy parmesan and freshly ground pepper.

Amount per (260 g) serving: Calories 170, Protein 5 g, Total Fat 13 g, Carbohydrates 10 g, Cholesterol 25 mg, Fiber 5 g, Saturated Fat 2 g, Sodium 320 mg, Sugar 3 g

> "I met my first Vitamix on Saturday, April 14, 2007, and it was love at first sight! It has been a lovefest ever since, and my Vitamix is the one thing in the kitchen that is always, always being used."
> MARILU HENNER

Raspberry Dijon Dressing

> **Before *organic foods* were popular, most Vitamix owners were people who cared about their health.** RANDALL WEISS

Preserve the Season

When fresh fruits or vegetables are in peak season, blend them into sauces and portion them into 1-cup containers for freezing. Enjoy fresh strawberry purée or tomato sauce all year 'round!

Intensify Flavors

The power of the Vitamix lets you use whole foods in their entirety and extract maximum flavor. For example, blend fresh herbs, nuts, and a splash of lemon juice into a fat-free green sauce that you can drizzle decoratively on the plate.

Dairy-Free

Transform raw, unsalted nuts into plant-based sauces that add richness and creamy texture without dairy.

SAUCES & SIDES

The Vitamix is a "must have" tool in restaurant kitchens all over the world. In the words of famed New York chef Marc Murphy, our commercial Vita-Prep is as essential to chefs as a paring knife.

Chefs tell us that they love their Vitamix products for their power, endurance, and versatility for making sauces and sides. They can "blitz" whole ingredients—skins, seeds, and all—to extract pure flavor that adds vibrancy to their dishes. With the Vitamix, they create silky smooth blends or emulsify sauces that don't separate. From smooth soups and sauces to fancy foams, chefs rely on the Vitamix to create, experiment, and set new trends.

That's why top chefs like Chris Cosentino, Jehangir Mehta, and others use the Vitamix to create the finest dishes that are celebrated around the world.

> **Although I've tried other brands of 'high powered' blenders, *nothing compares* to a Vitamix. Vitamix blenders produce an incredibly smooth product and velvety texture.** NAOMI POMEROY, FROM *TASTE AND TECHNIQUE*

If you're a fan of TV cooking shows, you'll easily spot Vitamix products being used by personalities like Alejandra Schrader and Laura Sandford, and on the set of top-rated programs like *Chopped*,® *Top Chef*,® and *Iron Chef*® *America*.

Just like these great chefs, you can use your Vitamix to create chef-inspired sauces and side dishes right in your own kitchen. For example, you can transform just a cup of whole cashews and a splash of lemon juice into a creamy, dairy-free sauce that adds tangy flavor to your family's favorite taco recipe. Using the Vitamix shows that you care about preparation and presentation by making something so simple and easy yet truly special—and, best of all, good for you!

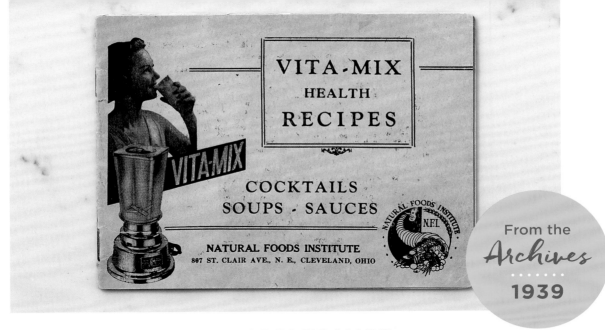

RAW APPLESAUCE

Shared by: Vitamix / *Published in:* 1939 / **48** **64** / 9 servings / *Total time:* 10 minutes

INGREDIENTS

6 medium apples (720 g), halved and seeded (peeled, if desired)

½ lemon, peeled

½ teaspoon ground cinnamon

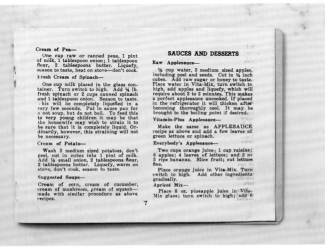

INSTRUCTIONS

Place all ingredients into the container in the order listed and secure the lid. Pulse the Vitamix on Variable 4–6, depending on desired texture, using the tamper to press ingredients toward the blades. Scrape down container as necessary and repeat until desired consistency is reached. For a fine purée, blend on the highest speed for 40–50 seconds.

Note: Lemon is optional and results in a lighter applesauce. For a cooked applesauce, place the blended mixture into a saucepan and simmer for 20–30 minutes.

Amount per (126 g) serving: Calories 60, Protein 0 g, Total Fat 0 g, Carbohydrates 17 g, Cholesterol 8 mg, Fiber 3 g, Saturated Fat 0 g, Sodium 1 mg, Sugar 13 g

Perhaps our oldest recipe! Grandma Ruth's Raw Applesauce appeared in one of the first cookbooks we published.

Vegan Cheese Sauce

VEGAN CHEESE SAUCE

Shared by: Breanna Pyrda, Vitamix Fan / **48** **64** / 12 servings / *Total time:* 25 minutes

INGREDIENTS

2 medium russet potatoes (300 g), cubed

2 large carrots (250 g), chopped

½ cup (120 ml) water

⅓ cup (80 ml) grapeseed oil

¼ lemon, peeled

½ cup (30 g) nutritional yeast

1 teaspoon Old Bay seasoning

1 teaspoon salt (optional)

½ teaspoon onion powder

½ teaspoon garlic powder

INSTRUCTIONS

Place potatoes and carrots in a saucepan with water to cover. Bring to a boil, then reduce heat and simmer until vegetables are fork-tender, about 20 minutes. Drain into a colander.

Place all ingredients into the container in the order listed and secure the lid. Start the Vitamix on its lowest speed, then quickly increase to its highest speed. Blend for 30 seconds or until smooth.

Enjoy immediately with tortilla chips or your favorite Mexican dishes, or refrigerate for up to 1 week. To reheat, simmer on low until sauce is heated through, or microwave for 45 seconds, stirring halfway through.

Amount per (67 g) serving: Calories 100, Protein 2 g, Total Fat 6 g, Carbohydrates 8 g, Cholesterol 1 mg, Fiber 2 g, Saturated Fat 1 g, Sodium 220 mg, Sugar 1 g

TAHINI

Shared by: Vitamix / *Published in:* 2005 / **48** **64** / 48 servings / *Total time:* 5 minutes

INGREDIENTS

5 cups (705 g) toasted sesame seeds

INSTRUCTIONS

Place sesame seeds into the container and secure the lid. Start the Vitamix on its lowest speed, then quickly increase to its highest speed. Blend for 2–3 minutes, using the tamper to press ingredients toward the blades.

Amount per (29 g) serving: Calories 210, Protein 8 g, Total Fat 16 g, Carbohydrates 4 g, Cholesterol 0 mg, Fiber 3 g, Saturated Fat 0 g, Sodium 40 mg, Sugar 0 g

MARINARA SAUCE

Shared by: Andrew Shaffer, Vitamix Recipe Assistant / **64** / 7 servings / *Total time:* 1 hour 10 minutes

INGREDIENTS

3 pounds (1.40 kg) Roma or plum tomatoes, stemmed

1 teaspoon olive oil

1 small yellow onion (140 g), peeled and diced

2 garlic cloves, peeled

2 sprigs fresh oregano

1 sprig fresh thyme

1 dried bay leaf

1 teaspoon tomato paste

3 fresh basil leaves

INSTRUCTIONS

Place tomatoes into the container and secure the lid. Start the Vitamix on its lowest speed, then quickly increase to its highest speed, using the tamper to press ingredients toward the blades. Blend for 1 minute.

In a large saucepan over medium heat, warm the olive oil. Add the onions and garlic and sauté until translucent, about 5 minutes. Add herb sprigs, bay leaf, and tomato paste, and cook for another 2 minutes.

Add the puréed tomatoes and bring to a simmer over medium heat. Cook for 1 hour. Let cool for 15 minutes. Remove herb sprigs and bay leaf.

Transfer the sauce to the container along with the basil leaves. Secure the lid. Blend on Variable 4 for 30 seconds. For a finer purée blend on the highest speed for 45 seconds.

Amount per (116 g) serving: Calories 50, Protein 2 g, Total Fat 1 g, Carbohydrates 10 g, Cholesterol 23 mg, Fiber 3 g, Saturated Fat 0 g, Sodium 10 mg, Sugar 6 g

TOMATO SAUCE FOR CANNING OR FREEZING

Shared by: Chris Applegate, Vitamix Fan / **32** **48** **64** / 8 servings / *Total time:* 1 hour

INGREDIENTS

3 pounds (1.40 kg) Roma or heirloom tomatoes, stemmed and halved

INSTRUCTIONS

Working in batches if necessary, place tomatoes into the container and secure the lid. Start the Vitamix on its lowest speed, then quickly increase to its highest speed. Blend for 2–3 minutes.

Transfer the tomato purée to a stock pot. Bring to a simmer over medium heat, then reduce heat to low and cook for about 45 minutes or until thickened.

To preserve the sauce, transfer to canning jars and process in a water-bath canner according to safe canning practices. Or transfer to freezer-safe containers and freeze for later use.

Amount per (122 g) serving: Calories 30, Protein 1 g, Total Fat 0 g, Carbohydrates 7 g, Cholesterol 5 mg, Fiber 2 g, Saturated Fat 0 g, Sodium 10 mg, Sugar 4 g

> "I grow and process a lot of tomatoes—about 40 quarts a year—and my Vitamix has made it so much easier."
> **CHRIS APPLEGATE**

Marinara Sauce

Vegan Walnut & Date Pesto

VEGAN WALNUT & DATE PESTO

Shared by: Alan Rudolph, Vitamix Project Manager, International Research

  / 4 servings / *Total time:* 10 minutes

INGREDIENTS

¼ cup (30 g) whole walnuts

8 Deglet Noor dates (60 g), pitted

2 Tablespoons extra-virgin olive oil

2 Tablespoons grated non-dairy parmesan cheese

8 sprigs flat-leaf parsley, leaves only

1 sprig fresh oregano, leaves only

½ sprig fresh rosemary, leaves only

1 garlic clove

INSTRUCTIONS

Place all ingredients into the Vitamix container in the order listed and secure the lid. Pulse 10–15 times on Variable 6, or until desired consistency is reached.

Amount per (40 g) serving: Calories 190, Protein 3 g, Total Fat 14 g, Carbohydrates 14 g, Cholesterol 10 mg, Fiber 2 g, Saturated Fat 2 g, Sodium 200 mg, Sugar 10 g

VEGAN GARLIC ALFREDO SAUCE

Shared by: John Alexander McFarlane, Vitamix Fan /   / 4 servings / *Total time:* 40 minutes

INGREDIENTS

2 medium white onions (400 g), peeled and sliced

3 cups (720 ml) vegetable broth, divided use

6 garlic cloves, peeled

¼ lemon, peeled

1 cup (140 g) whole roasted cashews

¼ cup (20 g) nutritional yeast

½ teaspoon salt (optional)

½ teaspoon ground black pepper

Add vegetable broth if you'd like a thinner consistency. Toss with freshly cooked whole wheat pasta or spoon over roasted vegetables.

INSTRUCTIONS

Combine onions and 2 cups of vegetable broth in a saucepan over medium heat. Simmer uncovered for 15–20 minutes or until the liquid is almost evaporated. Add the garlic cloves and reduce the heat to medium-low; simmer until all liquid has evaporated.

Pour the remaining 1 cup of vegetable broth into the Vitamix container. Add cooked onions and garlic, then remaining ingredients in the order listed and secure the lid. Start the Vitamix on its lowest speed, then quickly increase to its highest speed. Blend for 1–2 minutes, or until desired consistency is reached.

Amount per (118 g) serving: Calories 140, Protein 5 g, Total Fat 8 g, Carbohydrates 14 g, Cholesterol 6 mg, Fiber 2 g, Saturated Fat 2 g, Sodium 210 mg, Sugar 4 g

GARLICKY MASHED CAULIFLOWER

Shared by: Larry L., Vitamix Fan /   64 / 12 servings / *Total time:* 25 minutes

INGREDIENTS

1 head (580 g) cauliflower, broken into florets

3 garlic cloves, peeled

¼ cup (60 ml) **Soy Milk** (see page 176) or low-fat milk

¼ teaspoon salt (optional)

INSTRUCTIONS

Place cauliflower florets and garlic in a steamer basket and set over simmering water; cover and steam until fork tender, about 15–20 minutes. Drain into a colander and let sit for about 2 minutes.

Place the milk into the Vitamix container, followed by the cooked cauliflower and garlic, and secure the lid. Pulse on Variable 6, using the tamper to press ingredients toward the blades, until desired texture is reached. For a smooth, fine purée, blend on highest speed for 30–45 seconds.

Amount per (54 g) serving: Calories 15, Protein 1 g, Total Fat 0 g, Carbohydrates 3 g, Cholesterol 1 mg, Fiber 1 g, Saturated Fat 0 g, Sodium 10 mg, Sugar 1 g

CASHEW SOUR CREAM

Shared by: Brooke Nedrich, Vitamix Social Media Coordinator

  / 16 servings / *Total time:* 15 minutes

INGREDIENTS

1 cup (135 g) cashews

1 Tablespoon nutritional yeast

¼ small lemon, peeled

½ cup (120 ml) water

"I make this sour cream all the time when I want to spruce up dinner at home."
BROOKE NEDRICH

INSTRUCTIONS

Place all ingredients into the container in the order listed and secure the lid. Start the Vitamix on its lowest speed, then quickly increase to its highest speed. Blend for 3 minutes or until smooth and creamy. Chill thoroughly before enjoying.

Amount per (16 g) serving: Calories 40, Protein 1 g, Total Fat 3 g, Carbohydrates 2 g, Cholesterol 0 mg, Fiber 1 g, Saturated Fat 1 g, Sodium 2 mg, Sugar 1 g

Garlicky Mashed Cauliflower

"With my Vitamix, I'm able to make absolutely delicious plant-based recipes that are *packed with flavor* and nutrition, and are extremely easy to make! TAMARA DEGRASSE

SUPER HERBED FALAFEL

Shared by: Tamara DeGrasse, Vitamix Shows Sales Trainer

64 Low Profile / 5 servings / *Total time:* 9 hours

INGREDIENTS

1 cup (225 g) dried chickpeas

4 garlic cloves

1 cup (15 g) fresh cilantro leaves

12 sprigs flat-leaf parsley, leaves only

8 fresh mint leaves

6 sprigs fresh tarragon, leaves only

6 sprigs fresh oregano, leaves only

3 scallions (60 g), roots trimmed

¼ cup (20 g) sliced sweet onion

¾ teaspoon baking powder

1 teaspoon sea salt (optional)

1 teaspoon ground cumin

½ teaspoon dried basil

½ teaspoon onion powder

½ teaspoon ground coriander

½ teaspoon ground cardamom

¼ teaspoon ground cayenne pepper

1 teaspoon lime juice

INSTRUCTIONS

Rinse the chickpeas, then place in a large bowl and cover with cool water by 3–4 inches. Soak overnight or until beans are tripled in size. Drain chickpeas, rinse, then pat dry.

Place half the chickpeas, then the rest of the ingredients into the Vitamix container in the order listed, followed by the remaining half of the chickpeas. Secure the lid. Pulse the mixture on Variable 4 until ingredients are very finely chopped but not puréed, scraping down the container between pulses and using the tamper to press ingredients toward the blades. (If you can press a handful of the mixture together and it holds its shape, it is the correct texture.)

Transfer falafel mix to a bowl, cover and refrigerate for 20–30 minutes to help hold them together while frying. If making ahead, they can be stored in the refrigerator for up to 2 days.

Scoop out 1½ Tablespoons of the mixture and gently shape it into a ball, then place on a plate. Repeat with remaining mixture.

To bake: Preheat oven to 450°F (230°C); line a baking sheet with parchment. Place falafel balls onto baking sheet; bake for 15–20 minutes or until golden brown and heated through.

To fry: Add at least ¾ inch (2 cm) of grapeseed or avocado oil to a deep saucepan. Heat the oil over medium-high heat until it reaches 350°F (176°C). Working in batches, transfer falafel balls into the oil, turning occasionally and frying until golden brown on all sides. (Oil should bubble aggressively when falafel are added to ensure proper browning.) Transfer cooked falafel to a plate lined with paper towels, sprinkle with sea salt if desired.

Amount per (67 g) serving: Calories 60, Protein 3 g, Total Fat 1 g, Carbohydrates 10 g, Cholesterol 3 mg, Fiber 1 g, Saturated Fat 1 g, Sodium 200 mg, Sugar 2 g

HEARTS OF PALM CEVICHE

Shared by: Alejandra Schrader, a plant-based, nutrition-certified chef and food TV personality

  64 Classic / 6 servings / *Total time:* 1 hour

INGREDIENTS

For the marinated red onions:

½ cup (50 g) very thinly sliced red onion

3 Tablespoons (45 ml) fresh lime juice

Pinch of salt

1 teaspoon minced jalapeño (optional)

For the marinade:

½ cup (120 ml) coconut cream

¼ cup (60 ml) fresh lime juice

¼ cup (60 ml) passion fruit pulp and seeds

½ cup (10 g) cilantro stems

½ cup (10 g) celery leaves

2 Tablespoons sliced scallion, white parts only

2 garlic cloves, peeled

½ teaspoon sea salt (optional)

¼ teaspoon ground black pepper

1 ice cube

For the ceviche:

24 ounces hearts of palm, drained and sliced

¼ cup (40 g) minced celery

¼ cup (60 g) minced green bell pepper

¼ cup (5 g) fresh cilantro leaves, chopped

For serving: 1 sweet potato, cooked and sliced; 1 cup cooked corn; marinated red onions; thinly sliced Fresno peppers; cilantro leaves; lime wedges

INSTRUCTIONS

For the marinated onions: In a bowl, combine all ingredients; let sit 15 minutes, tossing occasionally.

For the marinade: Place all ingredients into the container in the order listed and secure the lid. Start the Vitamix on its lowest speed, then quickly increase to its highest speed. Blend for 1 minute.

For the ceviche: In a bowl, combine hearts of palm, celery, and green pepper; add marinade and toss to coat. Refrigerate for 30 minutes, mixing once. Add cilantro and toss to combine. Season to taste.

Divide ceviche among six serving bowls and garnish with sliced sweet potato, corn, marinated red onions, cilantro leaves, sliced peppers, and lime wedges.

Amount per (416 g) serving: Calories 300, Protein 7 g, Total Fat 5 g, Carbohydrates 61 g, Cholesterol 1 mg, Fiber 9 g, Saturated Fat 4 g, Sodium 740 mg, Sugar 35 g

> **My Vitamix helps us upcycle ingredients traditionally discarded and it marries them into a *perfectly smooth* flavor!**
> ALEJANDRA SCHRADER

SESAME ZUCCHINI WITH PARMESAN BASIL GANACHE

Shared by: Jehangir Mehta, owner of the New York restaurant Graffiti and runner-up on *The Next Iron Chef*®

  32 48 64 / 4 servings / *Total time:* 30 minutes

INGREDIENTS

For the ganache:

4 garlic cloves, peeled

4 cups (65 g) fresh basil leaves

½ cup (120 ml) olive oil

¼ cup (40 g) chickpeas

½ cup (50 g) Parmesan cheese

1 jalapeño, seeded

½ teaspoon salt (optional)

⅓ cup (80 ml) **Cashew Cream** (see page 175)

For the zucchini:

1 medium zucchini (350 g), thinly sliced

⅓ cup (30 g) sesame seeds

⅓ cup (80 ml) grapeseed oil

¼ teaspoon salt (optional)

INSTRUCTIONS

For the ganache: Place all ingredients except cream into the container in the order listed and secure the lid. Start the Vitamix on its lowest speed, then quickly increase to its highest speed, using the tamper to press ingredients toward the blades. Blend for 1 minute. Reduce speed to Variable 6 and remove lid plug. Slowly pour cream through the opening; replace lid plug and blend until combined.

For the zucchini: Place the sesame, grapeseed oil, and salt (if using) into the container and secure the lid. Start the Vitamix on its lowest speed, then quickly increase to Variable 6. Blend for 1 minute or until desired consistency is reached.

Place sliced zucchini in a bowl and add marinade; let sit for 5 minutes.

Place a smear of ganache on each serving plate and arrange zucchini over top. Drizzle with additional sesame marinade.

Amount per (209 g) serving: Calories 610, Protein 9 g, Total Fat 59 g, Carbohydrates 13 g, Cholesterol 10 mg, Fiber 3 g, Saturated Fat 9 g, Sodium 550 mg, Sugar 3 g

FRA DIAVOLO SAUCE

Shared by: Chris Cosentino, chef/co-owner of Cockscomb in San Francisco, among other restaurants

   / 32 servings / *Total time:* 10 minutes

INGREDIENTS

5 Tablespoons (28 g) Aleppo pepper

¼ cup (28 g) red pepper flakes

¼ cup (28 g) smoked Spanish paprika

3 Tablespoons (28 g) Tellicherry black peppercorns

3 Tablespoons (20 g) coriander seeds

1 Tablespoon white peppercorns

6 fresh bay leaves

15 garlic cloves

6 small serrano peppers (36 g), stemmed (seeded, if desired)

6 jalapeños (84 g), stemmed (seeded, if desired)

1¼ cups (50 g) fresh thyme leaves

3 Tablespoons grated orange zest

1 cup plus 1 teaspoon (280 ml) olive oil

INSTRUCTIONS

Place all dried spices and bay leaves into the container and secure the lid. Start the Vitamix on its lowest speed, then quickly increase to its highest speed. Blend for 30 seconds until all ingredients are pulverized.

Stop the Vitamix and remove lid. Add garlic cloves, chili peppers, thyme, orange zest, and olive oil. Secure the lid. Start the Vitamix on its lowest speed, then quickly increase to its highest speed. Blend for 30 seconds, using the tamper to press ingredients toward the blades, until desired consistency is reached.

Amount per (19 g) serving: Calories 90, Protein 1 g, Total Fat 9 g, Carbohydrates 2 g, Cholesterol 0 mg, Fiber 1 g, Saturated Fat 1 g, Sodium 10 mg, Sugar 0 g

This spicy sauce (the name means "brother devil" in Italian) is a great accompaniment to chicken, pork, or fish.

Batch It Up

It's so simple to make soup, especially when using the 64-ounce container, that you can quickly prepare a large batch to enjoy all week or freeze for later use.

Smart Seasoning

Wait to add seasoning—spices, pepper, lemon juice, or a pinch of salt—until after you've blended the soup. You'll be surprised how naturally flavorful whole foods are, which means you'll likely need to add less seasoning.

A Simple Ratio

When making soup, a rule of thumb is to fill the container with as many vegetables as you want then pour in water halfway to the top of the veggies.

Vitamix Does the Work

If using a Vitamix with program settings, add your ingredients to the container as noted in the recipe and select the Hot Soup setting. Your Vitamix will blend at the right speed and time to create a steaming hot soup.

SOUPS

I f you were to walk into the lunchroom here at Vitamix on any given workday, you'd find the usual scene: groups of employees sitting together having a meal and enjoying a break in their day. But you'd often find something unique to Vitamix: soup—whipped up moments before.

At our facilities around the world, we're fortunate to have Vitamix units for employees to use to make whatever they like. It's something my father, John, insisted upon—and he was right there too, sharing a table with all of us employees for lunch and conversation.

Vitamix Vegetable Soup (see facing page) is one of my favorites. Back in the day when a lunch break for me was not the luxury it is today, I would bring a bunch of vegetables and in just about 5 minutes, I would have a hot, hearty container of puréed deliciousness. I would walk through our Customer Care department doling out hot soup and visiting with my fellow employees. It was my Grandma Ruth who discovered the Vitamix superpower of generating heat from the sheer friction of the ingredients hitting the blades.

> **I use my Vitamix** *every day,* **starting in the morning to create matcha lattes. I also use it to create salad dressings, blended soups, and desserts.** ALISON WU

After blending, I like to stir in cooked beans or grains to add protein—you can also add seasonings of your choice, and sprinkle on garnishes like toasted seeds or fresh herbs.

Soup is the ultimate comfort food, and by making our own from scratch, we steer clear of the added sodium and artificial ingredients common in store-bought products. Plus, I cannot lie: There's something almost magical about feeding whole produce into the Vitamix and ladling out hot soup just moments later.

VEGETABLE SOUP

Shared by: Vitamix / *Published in:* 1992 / **64** / 2 servings / *Total time:* 15 minutes

INGREDIENTS

1 cup (240 ml) vegetable stock

2 Roma tomatoes (240 g)

2 celery stalks (100 g)

½ cup (60 g) frozen sweet peas, thawed

½ cup (90 g) frozen lima beans, thawed

1 small carrot (50 g)

1 slice green bell pepper (20 g)

1 garlic clove, peeled

¼ teaspoon onion powder

Pinch of ground black pepper

Pinch of salt (optional)

INSTRUCTIONS

Place all ingredients into the container in the order listed and secure the lid. Start the Vitamix on its lowest speed, then quickly increase to its highest speed. Blend for 5 minutes 45 seconds or until heavy steam escapes the vented lid.

Amount per (404 g) serving: Calories 130, Protein 7 g, Total Fat 1 g, Carbohydrates 26 g, Cholesterol 665 mg, Fiber 8 g, Saturated Fat 0 g, Sodium 530 mg, Sugar 8 g

From the
Archives
1992

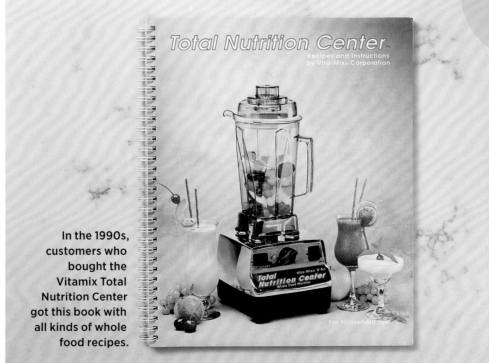

In the 1990s, customers who bought the Vitamix Total Nutrition Center got this book with all kinds of whole food recipes.

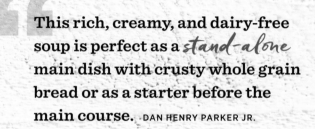

> This rich, creamy, and dairy-free soup is perfect as a *stand-alone* main dish with crusty whole grain bread or as a starter before the main course. —DAN HENRY PARKER JR.

HERB-INFUSED CREAMY SWEET ONION SOUP

Shared by: Dan Henry Parker Jr., founder of BlendingwithHenry.com and companion YouTube® channel

64 / 6 servings / *Total time:* 1 hour 30 minutes

INGREDIENTS

3 Tablespoons extra-virgin olive oil, divided use

1 medium Braeburn or Pink Lady apple (120 g), cored and chopped

4 garlic cloves, peeled and roasted

2 large yellow onions (400 g), sliced

3 parsnips (300 g), halved

¼ small avocado (35 g), pitted and peeled

⅓ cup (60 g) diced green bell pepper

4 cups (960 ml) vegetable broth

1 Tablespoon maple syrup

1 Tablespoon fresh thyme leaves, plus more for garnish

1 teaspoon red wine vinegar

Pinch of red pepper flakes

2 teaspoons salt (optional)

INSTRUCTIONS

Heat 1 Tablespoon of olive oil in a large skillet over medium heat; add chopped apples and sauté for 3–4 minutes or until golden. Add garlic and cook for 1–2 minutes more, until garlic is fragrant and browned. Transfer to the Vitamix container.

In the same skillet, heat remaining 2 Tablespoons of olive oil. Add onions. Cook over low heat until deeply golden and caramelized, 45–60 minutes, stirring often and adding a splash of water if the pan becomes too dry. Transfer caramelized onions to the Vitamix container.

Place remaining ingredients into the container in the order listed and secure the lid. Start the Vitamix on its lowest speed, then quickly increase to its highest speed. Blend for 5 minutes 45 seconds or until heavy steam escapes from the vented lid. Garnish with additional fresh thyme leaves.

Amount per (289 g) serving: Calories 150, Protein 1 g, Total Fat 8 g, Carbohydrates 19 g, Cholesterol 307 mg, Fiber 5 g, Saturated Fat 1 g, Sodium 730 mg, Sugar 8 g

SWEET POTATO POBLANO SOUP

Shared by: Laine Pickrel, Vitamix Fan /   / 4 servings / *Total time:* 40 minutes

INGREDIENTS

2 sweet potatoes (730 g), peeled and
cut into 2-inch pieces

1 large yellow onion (230 g), peeled and diced

3 poblano peppers (195 g), seeded and quartered

2 garlic cloves, peeled

1½ cups (360 ml) water

1½ cups (360 ml) **Coconut Milk** (see page 175)

1 cup (30 g) baby spinach

INSTRUCTIONS

Place sweet potatoes, onion, poblano peppers, garlic, and water in a saucepan and cook for 10 minutes. Add coconut milk and bring to a brisk simmer. Cook for 15 minutes, or until sweet potatoes are tender, then remove from heat and allow to cool for 10 minutes.

Transfer mixture to the container and secure the lid. Start the Vitamix on its lowest speed, then quickly increase to its highest speed. Blend for 2 minutes.

Carefully pour the puréed soup back into the pan. Set over low heat and add the spinach, stirring it in and allowing it to wilt.

Amount per (452 g) serving: Calories 340, Protein 6 g, Total Fat 14 g, Carbohydrates 49 g, Cholesterol 11 mg, Fiber 8 g, Saturated Fat 14 g, Sodium 135 mg, Sugar 14 g

CREAMY VEGAN SOUP BASE

Shared by: Rhonda Legge, Vitamix Demonstrator, Canada /   / 2 servings / *Total time:* 15 minutes

INGREDIENTS

¼ cup (45 g) uncooked white rice or lentils

¼ cup (20 g) unsweetened shredded coconut

1 vegetable bouillon cube

2 cups (480 ml) water

This is a base that can be used to create many kinds of soup. Try adding sweet onions and Indian spices, carrots and ginger, cooked mushrooms and onions, or any of your favorite soup ingredients.

INSTRUCTIONS

Place all ingredients into the container in the order listed and secure the lid. Start the Vitamix on its lowest speed, then quickly increase to its highest speed. Blend for 5 minutes 30 seconds or until heavy steam escapes from vented lid.

Amount per (275 g) serving: Calories 150, Protein 2 g, Total Fat 6 g, Carbohydrates 21 g, Cholesterol 1 mg, Fiber 3 g, Saturated Fat 5 g, Sodium 490 mg, Sugar 1 g

*Sweet Potato
Poblano Soup*

Carrot Ginger Soup

CARROT GINGER SOUP

Shared by: Jen Picciano, reporter for WOIO-TV and creator of the food segment "Cleveland Cooks"

64 / 2 servings / *Total time:* 15 minutes

INGREDIENTS

3 large carrots (350 g), halved and cut into chunks

1 (½-inch thick) slice yellow onion (20 g), peeled

1 (½-inch thick) slice fresh ginger (8 g), chopped

1 garlic clove, peeled and chopped

1 Tablespoon olive oil

2 cups (480 ml) vegetable stock

2 teaspoons salt (optional)

¼ teaspoon ground black pepper

Pinch of turmeric

¼ cup (60 ml) **Coconut Milk** (see page 175) or coconut cream

INSTRUCTIONS

Preheat oven to 350°F. On a rimmed baking sheet, toss carrots, onion, ginger, and garlic with olive oil to coat. Roast until tender.

Place roasted vegetables and remaining ingredients into the container and secure the lid. Start the Vitamix on its lowest speed, then quickly increase to its highest speed. Blend for 5 minutes 45 seconds, or until heavy steam escapes from the vented lid. When soup is steaming, lower to Variable 3 and remove lid plug. Pour in the coconut milk. Replace lid plug and blend for another 10 seconds.

Amount per (310 g) serving: Calories 90, Protein 2 g, Total Fat 5 g, Carbohydrates 13 g, Cholesterol 0 mg, Fiber 4 g, Saturated Fat 4 g, Sodium 1630 mg, Sugar 6 g

CREAMY MUSHROOM SOUP

Shared by: Lance Roetling, Vitamix Fan / **64** / 3 servings / *Total time:* 15 minutes

INGREDIENTS

2 cups (280 g) roasted cremini mushrooms

2 cups (480 ml) hot water or vegetable stock

1 garlic clove, peeled

1 small avocado (140 g), halved, pitted, and peeled

¼ teaspoon salt (optional)

¼ teaspoon ground black pepper

1 cup (30 g) fresh spinach

INSTRUCTIONS

Place all ingredients except spinach into the container in the order listed and secure the lid. Start the Vitamix on its lowest speed, then quickly increase to its highest speed. Blend for 5 minutes 45 seconds or until heavy steam escapes from the vented lid. When soup is steaming, lower to Variable 3 and remove lid plug. Add the spinach. Replace lid plug and blend for another 10 seconds.

Amount per (301 g) serving: Calories 100, Protein 3 g, Total Fat 7 g, Carbohydrates 9 g, Cholesterol 2 mg, Fiber 5 g, Saturated Fat 1 g, Sodium 210 mg, Sugar 2 g

"The Vitamix has made it easy for me to provide my family fresh, healthy options and also saves me money."
LANCE ROETLING

> **Our most popular recipe! The Vitamix creates the *creamy texture,* and our childhood memories inspired the flavor.**
>
> SHALVA AND LENNY GALE

CREAMY WILD RICE SOUP

Shared by: Shalva and Lenny Gale, Vitamix affiliate partners, LifeIsNoYoke.com

32 **48** **64** / 4 servings / *Total time:* 1 hour

INGREDIENTS

1 cup (125 g) raw cashews

8 cups (2 l) vegetable broth, divided use

1 (15 ounce, 425 g) can cannellini beans, drained

1 cup (160 g) wild rice, rinsed and drained

3 celery stalks (180 g), chopped

1 large carrot (100 g), chopped

½ medium yellow onion (80 g), peeled and chopped

5 garlic cloves, peeled and chopped

1 Tablespoon dried thyme

2 dried bay leaves

2 teaspoons salt (optional)

8 ounces (225 g) mushrooms, chopped or sliced

INSTRUCTIONS

Soak cashews in water to cover overnight or in boiling water for 10 minutes; drain. Place cashews, cannellini beans, and 1 cup vegetable broth into the container and secure the lid. Start the Vitamix on its lowest speed, then quickly increase to its highest speed. Blend for 1 minute.

Heat the remaining 7 cups vegetable broth in large saucepan or stock pot over medium heat. When broth comes to a boil, add wild rice, celery, carrot, onion, garlic, thyme, and bay leaves. Cover and cook over medium heat for 30 minutes.

Add cashew-bean mixture to vegetables; stir to combine. Add mushrooms and cook, uncovered, for 15 minutes. Remove the bay leaves; taste and adjust seasoning.

Amount per (411 g) serving: Calories 250, Protein 9 g, Total Fat 7 g, Carbohydrates 36 g, Cholesterol 5 mg, Fiber 6 g, Saturated Fat 1 g, Sodium 880 mg, Sugar 6 g

CREAMY BROCCOLI SOUP

Shared by: Alison Wu, author of the holistic lifestyle blog WuHaus.com

 / 7 servings / *Total time:* 40 minutes

INGREDIENTS

¼ cup (60 ml) olive oil, divided use

1 medium yellow onion (120 g), peeled and chopped

3 garlic cloves, peeled and chopped

Zest of 1 lemon

2 pounds (900 g) broccoli, roughly chopped

1 teaspoon red pepper flakes, or to taste

4 cups (960 ml) low-sodium vegetable broth

5 cups (150 g) fresh spinach

1 cup (140 g) whole raw cashews, soaked in water until softened, if desired

2 Tablespoons nutritional yeast

1 teaspoon salt (optional)

½ teaspoon ground black pepper

INSTRUCTIONS

In a heavy pot, heat 2 Tablespoons of olive oil over medium heat. Once oil is hot, add onion, garlic, and lemon zest; season with salt and black pepper. Sauté for 5–7 minutes, until the onion starts to turn translucent. Add the broccoli and remaining 2 Tablespoons olive oil, tossing to coat. Sauté for 3–5 minutes, uncovered, stirring occasionally. Add the red pepper flakes; cover and cook 5 minutes more.

Uncover and add the broth, spinach, cashews, and nutritional yeast. Season to taste with salt and pepper, if desired. Bring to a simmer over medium heat, then reduce heat slightly and gently simmer for about 15 minutes or until broccoli is tender.

Carefully transfer soup to the container and secure the lid. Start the Vitamix on its lowest speed, then quickly increase to its highest speed, using the tamper to press ingredients toward the blades. Blend for 1 minute or until desired consistency is reached.

Amount per (303 g) serving: Calories 230, Protein 8 g, Total Fat 15 g, Carbohydrates 16 g, Cholesterol 3 mg, Fiber 5 g, Saturated Fat 3 g, Sodium 135 mg, Sugar 4 g

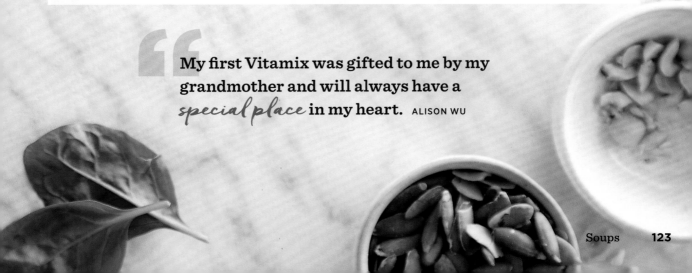

My first Vitamix was gifted to me by my grandmother and will always have a *special place* in my heart. ALISON WU

AVOCADO SOUP

Shared by: Mads Bo, Vitamix Distributor, Denmark /   / 3 servings / *Total time:* 15 minutes

INGREDIENTS

½ lemon

2 medium avocados (350 g), halved, pitted, and peeled

¾ cup (100 g) frozen sweet peas, thawed

½ medium cucumber (100 g)

½ bunch fresh mint leaves (3 g)

½ bunch fresh basil leaves (5 g)

2 garlic cloves, peeled

¼ teaspoon cayenne

½ cup (120 ml) **Soy Milk** (see page 176)

¾ cup (180 ml) water

¼ teaspoon salt (optional)

¼ teaspoon ground black pepper

INSTRUCTIONS

Use a microplane or grater to zest the lemon. With a peeler or paring knife, remove the bitter white pith (optional). Add the zest and fruit to the Vitamix container. Place all remaining ingredients into the container in the order listed and secure the lid. Start the Vitamix on its lowest speed, then quickly increase to its highest speed, using the tamper to press ingredients toward the blades. Blend for 40–50 seconds or until desired consistency is reached. Season to taste. To thin the soup, add soy milk or water.

Amount per (300 g) serving: Calories 260, Protein 6 g, Total Fat 19 g, Carbohydrates 20 g, Cholesterol 1 mg, Fiber 10 g, Saturated Fat 3 g, Sodium 270 mg, Sugar 4 g

TOMATO BELL PEPPER SOUP

Shared by: Janae Jensen, Vitamix Sales Rep /   Low Profile / 3 servings / *Total time:* 35 minutes

INGREDIENTS

8 Roma tomatoes (500 g)

1 medium red bell pepper (150 g), quartered and seeded

5 garlic cloves, peeled

½ medium yellow onion (100 g), peeled and halved

6 fresh basil leaves

¼ cup (20 g) grated Parmesan cheese or soy parmesan

1¼ cups (300 ml) vegetable or chicken broth

¼ cup (60 ml) **Cashew Cream** (see page 175) or heavy cream

¼ teaspoon ground black pepper

¼ teaspoon salt (optional)

INSTRUCTIONS

Preheat oven to 400°F (205°C). Place tomatoes, bell pepper, garlic cloves, and yellow onion on a parchment-lined baking sheet and sprinkle with salt and pepper if desired. Roast for 20 minutes or until tender.

Place all ingredients into the container in the order listed and secure the lid. Start the Vitamix on its lowest speed, then quickly increase to its highest speed, using the tamper to press ingredients toward the blades. Blend for 3 minutes or until heavy steam escapes from vented lid.

Amount per (310 g) serving: Calories 150, Protein 7 g, Total Fat 6 g, Carbohydrates 19 g, Cholesterol 5 mg, Fiber 4 g, Saturated Fat 2 g, Sodium 190 mg, Sugar 9 g

ALLY'S ASPARAGUS SOUP

Shared by: Ally Fazzalaro, Vitamix Territory Sales Manager / **64** / 5 servings / *Total time:* 30 minutes

INGREDIENTS

1 pound (454 g) asparagus, ends trimmed

1 Tablespoon extra-virgin olive oil

2 medium avocados (260 g), halved, pitted, and peeled (reserve 1 for garnish)

2½ cups (600 ml) water

1½ cups (360 ml) **Coconut Milk** (see page 175) or coconut cream

1 vegetable bouillon cube

2 cups (60 g) fresh spinach

1 garlic clove, peeled

Pinch of salt (optional)

Pinch of ground black pepper

INSTRUCTIONS

Preheat oven to 400°F; line a rimmed baking sheet with parchment. Arrange asparagus in a single layer on baking sheet and drizzle with olive oil; season with salt and pepper. Roast for 12–14 minutes or until tender. If desired, cut off tops and reserve for garnish.

Place all ingredients except second avocado into the container in the order listed and secure the lid. Start the Vitamix on its lowest speed, then quickly increase to its highest speed. Blend for 5 minutes 30 seconds or until heavy steam escapes from vented lid.

Portion into bowls and garnish with reserved asparagus tops, slices of reserved avocado, and freshly ground black pepper.

Amount per (310 g) serving: Calories 44, Protein 3 g, Total Fat 24 g, Carbohydrates 56 g, Cholesterol 1 mg, Fiber 5 g, Saturated Fat 16 g, Sodium 310 mg, Sugar 48 g

> **We have had a Vitamix since 2002.** *We love it* **so much that both my husband and I have worked for Vitamix since 2002 and 2005.** JANAE JENSEN

DIY Flour

Quickly make your own whole grain flour in your Vitamix to add a special flavor and freshness to quick breads and cookies. See page 30 for a Grain Grinding chart.

. . . .

Vegan Variation

To replace egg in batters, substitute a flax seed "slurry." Grind whole flax seed in the Vitamix to a powder, then whisk together 1 tablespoon of flax meal and 3 tablespoons of water; let sit to thicken (equivalent to 1 whole egg).

Sweet & Healthy

Lose the refined sugar without sacrificing taste by substituting dates or date syrup, honey, applesauce, or molasses.

QUICK BREADS & COOKIES

Imagine welcoming your child home from school with a plate of warm cookies—fragrant with cinnamon and ginger—and made with whole wheat flour and no dairy, oil, or egg. What a joy to begin your weekend with homemade whole grain pancakes with fruit compote. With your Vitamix, you can quickly and easily create healthy, whole food baked goods for those you love.

Compared to the refined flours common in store-bought breads and cookies, freshly ground whole grain flour is loaded with nutrition: fiber, antioxidants, and vitamins. You can transform wheat berries, oats, or gluten-free grains into flour in a quick minute with your Vitamix. (See the Whole Wheat Flour recipe on page 177.)

When I was a growing up, our annual Barnard family gatherings included a talent show. When the family grew to nearly 30 strong, we moved from my grandparents' humble home to the Vitamix headquarters. One time during the performance, I heard a phone ring throughout the building, and watched as my Grandpa Bill left his seat to answer it. I'll admit I was a little peeved: He was skipping the talent show! Taking a call on a weekend! I followed him and listened in as he patiently walked the caller through the process of making whole grain bread in her Vitamix.

> Going grain free can be a challenge, but my Vitamix has made it so much easier! From pancake batter to muffin mixes, it is *so helpful* for those of us with food sensitivities and allergies. KIRAN DODEJA SMITH

That lesson taught me a lot about what customer care really means and says so much about my Grandpa and his devotion to serving our customers, no matter what. But just as important, this happened over 40 years ago—demonstrating that our passion for being more than a blender has always been part of our company fiber (pun intended!).

I have made hearty bread, quick pancake batter, cookies, and so much more with all kinds of homemade flours and whole food ingredients. One tradition I especially enjoy is making whole wheat cranberry bread to give as gifts for the holiday. I whip up a loaf in minutes and am always delighted when people request it again the following year. Let the Vitamix be your secret ingredient to creating your own simple and scrumptious traditions.

WHOLE WHEAT BREAD

Shared by: Vitamix / *Published in:* 2010 / **48** **64** / 12 servings / *Total time:* 1 hour 20 minutes

INGREDIENTS

1¼ cups (300 ml) water, 105°F–115°F (40°C–46°C)

1 Tablespoon honey

1 (¼ ounce, 7 g) package active dry yeast

2¾ cups (390 g) **Whole Wheat Flour** (see page 177)

1 teaspoon salt (optional)

1 Tablespoon extra-virgin olive oil

1 teaspoon fresh lemon juice

1 large egg white beaten with 1 Tablespoon water, for finishing (optional)

INSTRUCTIONS

In a bowl, combine warm water, honey, and yeast; stir to dissolve yeast and honey. Let sit until the surface of the mixture becomes foamy (this may take up to 30 minutes).

Place the flour and salt into the container and secure the lid. Start the Vitamix on its lowest speed and increase speed to Variable 6. Blend until a hole forms in the center of the mixture, about 5 seconds. Turn the Vitamix off and remove lid plug.

Pour oil, lemon juice, and yeast mixture into the hole in the flour. Secure lid plug. Select Variable 6 and pulse 5–6 times. Remove the lid. Use a nylon spatula to scrape the sides of the container. Pull the dough away from the container sides and toward the center. Select the highest setting and pulse 5–6 times.

Repeat the above two-step process two times, or until a soft, elastic dough forms. Invert the container over a lightly floured cutting board to release the dough. Knead the dough until smooth.

Lightly coat an 8½-inch x 4½-inch (22 cm x 11 cm) loaf pan with cooking spray. Press the dough into a rectangle, then roll up into a tight cylinder. Pinch the seam to seal. Tuck the ends under; pinch to seal. Place dough seam-side down into prepared pan.

Allow the dough to rise in a warm (ideally 90°F/ 32°C) place, uncovered, until the top of it reaches the top of the pan, about 25–30 minutes. Preheat oven to 350°F (180°C).

If desired, brush the loaf gently with the egg-water mixture. Use a sharp serrated knife to make three to four diagonal slits about ¼-inch (.6 cm) deep across the top of the loaf.

Bake for 35 minutes or until the bread is well browned and reaches an internal temperature of 200°F (93°C) when tested with an instant-read thermometer. Cool on a wire rack for 10 minutes, then carefully remove from the pan and allow to cool completely before slicing.

Amount per (57 g) serving: Calories 120, Protein 4 g, Total Fat 2 g, Carbohydrates 24 g, Cholesterol 0 mg, Fiber 4 g, Saturated Fat 0 g, Sodium 190 mg, Sugar 1 g

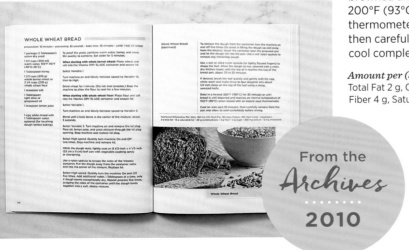

From the *Archives* 2010

This whole wheat bread recipe is a family favorite that has been published in various Vitamix cookbooks, including our 2010 *Whole Grains Cookbook*.

Zucchini Pancakes

ZUCCHINI PANCAKES

Shared by: Vitamix / *Published in:* 1996 / **64** Low Profile / 8 servings / *Total time:* 25 minutes

INGREDIENTS

⅓ cup (80 ml) **Almond Milk** (see page 175)

1¼ medium zucchini (250 g), peeled and halved

2 large eggs

¼ teaspoon salt (optional)

3 Tablespoons (60 g) **Date Syrup** (see page 176) or honey

1 Tablespoon ground cinnamon

¼ teaspoon ground allspice

1½ cups (180 g) **Whole Wheat Flour** (see page 177)

2 teaspoons baking powder

INSTRUCTIONS

Place all ingredients except for flour and baking powder into the container in the order listed and secure the lid. Start the Vitamix on its lowest speed, then increase to Variable 4. Blend for 5 seconds until ingredients are combined. Add the flour and baking powder to the container and secure the lid. Pulse 10–12 times on Variable 5 until ingredients are well incorporated.

Preheat a large skillet or griddle and grease lightly. Scoop ¼ cup of batter into the pan, cooking until small bubbles appear toward the center of each pancake before flipping gently. Cook another 2 minutes until cooked through. Repeat with remaining batter.

Amount per (87 g) serving: Calories 130, Protein 5 g, Total Fat 2 g, Carbohydrates 23 g, Cholesterol 45 mg, Fiber 3 g, Saturated Fat 1 g, Sodium 105 mg, Sugar 6 g

SOFT GINGER COOKIES

Shared by: Vitamix / *Published in:* 1975 / **48** **64** / 24 cookies / *Total time:* 40 minutes

INGREDIENTS

½ cup (120 ml) **Raw Applesauce** (see page 95)

3 Tablespoons (40 g) plant-based margarine

¾ cup (180 ml) dark molasses

¾ cup (180 ml) water

1 teaspoon baking soda

1 teaspoon baking powder

½ teaspoon salt (optional)

½ teaspoon ground allspice

½ teaspoon ground cloves

½ teaspoon ground cinnamon

¼ teaspoon ground ginger

3 cups (360 g) **Whole Wheat Flour** (see page 177) or all-purpose flour

INSTRUCTIONS

Place all ingredients except flour into the container in the order listed and secure the lid. Start the Vitamix on its lowest speed and blend for 5 seconds to combine. In three additions, add the flour to the container, pulsing after each addition to incorporate the flour, using the tamper to press ingredients toward the blades.

Transfer the dough to a bowl and cover; refrigerate for 20–30 minutes. Preheat oven to 350°F (180°C); lightly spray a baking sheet with cooking spray. Drop dough by rounded spoonfuls onto the prepared baking sheet. Bake for 12–14 minutes or until firm.

Amount per (38 g) serving: Calories 80, Protein 2 g, Total Fat 0 g, Carbohydrates 19 g, Cholesterol 6 mg, Fiber 2 g, Saturated Fat 0 g, Sodium 105 mg, Sugar 8 g

APPLESAUCE COOKIES

Shared by: Vitamix / *Published in:* 1975 / **64** / 16 cookies / *Total time:* 50 minutes

INGREDIENTS

1 cup (115 g) walnuts

1 cup (160 g) raisins

2 cups (245 g) **Whole Wheat Flour** (see page 129) or all-purpose flour

1 teaspoon baking soda

½ teaspoon salt (optional)

½ teaspoon ground cloves

½ teaspoon ground cinnamon

¼ teaspoon ground nutmeg

1½ cups (360 ml) **Raw Applesauce** (see page 95)

3 Tablespoons (45 ml) flax seed slurry or 1 large egg

INSTRUCTIONS

Preheat oven to 350°F (180°C). Line a baking sheet with parchment.

Place walnuts and raisins into the Vitamix container and secure the lid. Select Variable 5. Pulse 4–5 times. Transfer mixture to a bowl. In another bowl, combine flour, baking soda, salt (if using), and spices.

Place applesauce and slurry or egg into the Vitamix container and secure the lid. Pulse on the lowest setting until combined. Add about one-third of the flour mixture. Select Variable 5 and pulse to combine. Scrape down the sides of the container, then add another one-third of flour mixture and pulse to combine. Repeat with remaining flour mixture.

Transfer dough to the bowl with the walnuts and raisins and mix to incorporate. Drop dough by rounded spoonfuls onto the prepared baking sheet. Bake for 15 minutes, or until golden brown. Transfer to a wire rack to cool completely.

Amount per (59 g) serving: Calories 140, Protein 4 g, Total Fat 6 g, Carbohydrates 23 g, Cholesterol 10 mg, Fiber 3 g, Saturated Fat 1 g, Sodium 160 mg, Sugar 8 g

GRANDPA'S PANCAKES

Shared by: John Barnard, Vitamix Executive Chairman / **48** **64** / 14 servings / *Total time:* 25 minutes

INGREDIENTS

1 cup (180 g) wheat berries

1 cup (175 g) steel-cut oats

1½ cups (340 g) almond yogurt or plain yogurt

1 cup (120 g) **Cornmeal** (see page 177)

1½ teaspoons baking soda

1 teaspoon vanilla extract

1 cup (240 ml) water or **Almond Milk** (see page 175)

INSTRUCTIONS

Place the wheat berries and oats into the container and secure the lid. Start the Vitamix on its lowest speed, then quickly increase to its highest speed. Blend for 1 minute or until grains are finely processed. Add remaining ingredients to the container in the order listed and secure the lid. Pulse on Variable 4, using the tamper to press ingredients toward the blades until combined. (The batter should be pourable; if too thick, add water.)

Preheat a large skillet or griddle and grease lightly. Scoop ¼ cup of batter into the pan, cooking until small bubbles appear toward the center of each pancake before flipping gently. Cook another 2 minutes until cooked through. Repeat with remaining batter.

Amount per (301 g) serving: Calories 100, Protein 3 g, Total Fat 7 g, Carbohydrates 9 g, Cholesterol 2 mg, Fiber 5 g, Saturated Fat 1 g, Sodium 210 mg, Sugar 2 g

*Applesauce
Cookies*

Flourless Blueberry
Banana Muffins

FLOURLESS BLUEBERRY BANANA MUFFINS

Shared by: TLP120, Vitamix Fan / **64** Low Profile / 12 muffins / *Total time:* 40 minutes

INGREDIENTS

¼ cup (60 ml) **Almond Milk** (see page 175)

2 medium bananas (240 g), peeled

½ cup (120 ml) **Raw Applesauce** (see page 95)

2 large eggs

½ cup (120 ml) maple syrup, or 6 dates, pitted

½ cup (120 ml) **Almond Butter** (see page 174)

1 Tablespoon vanilla extract

2¼ cups (180 g) rolled oats

1 teaspoon baking powder

½ teaspoon baking soda

¼ teaspoon salt (optional)

½ cup (75 g) blueberries

INSTRUCTIONS

Preheat oven to 350°F (180°C). Lightly grease a 12-cup muffin pan or line with paper liners.

Place all ingredients except blueberries into the container in the order listed and secure the lid. Start the Vitamix on its lowest speed, then quickly increase to its highest speed. Blend for 30 seconds or until smooth.

Transfer batter to a bowl, then gently fold in blueberries. Spoon batter into prepared pan, filling each cup three-quarters full. Bake for 20 minutes, until tops are lightly golden brown and a toothpick inserted into the center of a muffin comes out with just a few moist crumbs. Cool for 10–15 minutes.

Amount per (57 g) serving: Calories 190, Protein 5 g, Total Fat 7 g, Carbohydrates 28 g, Cholesterol 9 mg, Fiber 3 g, Saturated Fat 1 g, Sodium 130 mg, Sugar 14 g

FLOURLESS PUMPKIN MUFFINS

Shared by: Kiran Dodeja Smith, Vitamix Fan / **64** Low Profile / 12 muffins / *Total time:* 30 minutes

INGREDIENTS

⅔ cup (160 g) pumpkin purée

½ cup (120 ml) **Raw Applesauce** (see page 95)

2 medium bananas (240 g), peeled

1 cup (265 g) **Peanut Butter** (see page 174)

1 teaspoon baking powder

⅔ cup (150 g) dark chocolate chips, or ½ cup (50 g) cocoa nibs

INSTRUCTIONS

Preheat oven to 375°F (190°C). Lightly grease a 12-cup muffin pan or line with paper liners.

Place all ingredients except chocolate chips into the container in the order listed and secure the lid. Start the Vitamix on its lowest speed, then quickly increase to its highest speed, using the tamper as necessary to press ingredients toward the blades. Blend for 10 seconds. Add the chocolate chips, select Variable 1. Pulse 4–5 times, using the tamper to press ingredients toward the blades.

Spoon batter into prepared pan, filling each cup three-quarters full. Bake for 18–20 minutes, until tops are lightly golden brown and a toothpick inserted into the center of a muffin comes out with just a few moist crumbs. Cool for 10–15 minutes.

Amount per (64 g) serving: Calories 220, Protein 6 g, Total Fat 15 g, Carbohydrates 20 g, Cholesterol 3 mg, Fiber 2 g, Saturated Fat 4 g, Sodium 150 mg, Sugar 10 g

Use the Tamper

The tamper is helpful in creating the perfect blend when using frozen ingredients. As needed, use it to push ingredients toward the blades to keep the mixture flowing.

Visual Cues

When you're making a frozen dessert, watch the container: When it is finished, you'll see four distinct mounds at the top of the blend. Stop the Vitamix to avoid melting the mixture.

Blending Frozen Foods

Don't be afraid to add frozen ingredients to your Vitamix—it was designed to handle them and will create a silky-smooth blend.

One-Touch Blending

If making a frozen treat in a Vitamix with program settings, add your ingredients to the container as the recipe directs and select the Frozen Dessert setting. Delicious, frosty perfection!

DESSERTS & TREATS

Who says decadence can't be healthy? If you've happened upon one of our wonderful demonstrators showcasing the Vitamix's versatility, you know that our frozen desserts are a real showstopper. People are delighted when, like magic, fruits and *vegetables* (yes, we add veggies and call it "stealth health") are transformed into the most delicious frozen treat. Kids beg for more and parents realize in that moment that the Vitamix is the right tool to bring whole food goodness home to the family kitchen.

Like it did my grandfather, it distresses me that so many people think healthy eating is all about deprivation—no dessert allowed. Nothing could be further from the truth!

Frozen fruit like strawberries, melons, peaches, you name it, quickly turn into a creamy sorbet. Add dairy to transform the blend into ice cream— but if you want to avoid dairy, whole raw cashews work like a charm. Of course, you can blend up non-frozen desserts like chocolate pudding that gets its richness from—would you believe— avocado! Or freeze your morning smoothie in popsicle molds. Parents love sneaking healthy foods like avocado, spinach, and carrots into tasty treats kids eagerly dig into.

> "My family has used Vitamix for over *60 years,* and as my children got older I bought them their own. I use mine for making green smoothies, soups, and healthy desserts. I wouldn't be without it! CINDY CHANDLER

The Vitamix headquarters is surrounded by a tree-filled residential neighborhood, and back in my grandfather's day, local kids knew that they could persuade him to take them into the test kitchen, and they would watch with amazement as he blended up a batch of strawberry sherbet. He was always happy to oblige, knowing that the healthy snack wouldn't spoil their dinners.

To this day, the Vitamix creates desserts that are just the right kind of indulgent: full of vibrant, scrumptious flavor, and bursting with nutrition that nourishes your friends and family.

Complete

Recipes & Instructions

for easy, healthful and wholesome Gourmet Cooking with

VITAMIX® 3600

INSTANT BLADE REVERSAL

From the *Archives* 1977

Everyone raves about this two-ingredient frozen treat! The recipe originated in Vitamix's "gourmet cooking" booklet.

STRAWBERRY YOGURT FREEZE

Shared by: Vitamix / *Published in:* 1977 / **48** **64** Classic / 4 servings / *Total time:* 10 minutes

INGREDIENTS

1 cup (240 ml) non-dairy yogurt or vanilla yogurt

1 pound (454 g) frozen strawberries

INSTRUCTIONS

Place all ingredients into the container in the order listed and secure lid. Start the Vitamix on its lowest speed, then quickly increase to its highest speed, using the tamper to press ingredients toward the blades. In about 30–60 seconds, the sound of the motor will change and four mounds should form in the mixture. Stop the Vitamix. Do not overblend, or the mixture will melt. Serve immediately.

Amount per (104 g) serving: Calories 60, Protein 2 g, Total Fat 1 g, Carbohydrates 11 g, Cholesterol 5 mg, Fiber 1 g, Saturated Fat 0 g, Sodium 25 mg, Sugar 8 g

DAIRY-FREE AÇAÍ BOWL

Shared by: Debra Kaplan, Vitamix Fan / / 8 servings / *Total time:* 10 minutes

INGREDIENTS

1 cup (240 ml) **Oat Milk** (see page 175)

2 cups (60 g) fresh spinach

1 Tablespoon pea protein powder

1 Tablespoon flax seed

1 Tablespoon sunflower seeds

3 dates (45 g), pitted

2 dried figs (30 g)

2 Sambazon açaí bars (200 g), halved, or 2 cups frozen blueberries

2 frozen bananas (250 g), peeled and halved

INSTRUCTIONS

Place all ingredients into the container in the order listed and secure the lid. Start the Vitamix on its lowest speed, then quickly increase to its highest speed, using the tamper to press ingredients toward the blades. In about 30–60 seconds, the sound of the motor will change and four mounds should form in the mixture. Stop the Vitamix. Do not overblend or mixture will melt. Serve immediately.

Amount per (105 g) serving: Calories 100, Protein 5 g, Total Fat 2 g, Carbohydrates 18 g, Cholesterol 4 mg, Fiber 2 g, Saturated Fat 0 g, Sodium 30 mg, Sugar 13 g

MANGO NICE CREAM

Shared by: Tami Cockrell, Vitamix Fan / / 6 servings / *Total time:* 10 minutes

INGREDIENTS

4 cups (500 g) frozen mango chunks

¼ cup (60 ml) maple syrup or pitted dates

Garnish with sliced mango and mint, as shown on our beautiful cover.

INSTRUCTIONS

Place all ingredients into the container in the order listed and secure the lid. Start the Vitamix on its lowest speed, then quickly increase to its highest speed, using the tamper to press ingredients toward the blades. In about 30–60 seconds, the sound of the motor will change and four mounds should form in the mixture. Stop the Vitamix. Do not overblend or mixture will melt. Serve immediately.

Amount per (97 g) serving: Calories 90, Protein 1 g, Total Fat 0 g, Carbohydrates 23 g, Cholesterol 17 mg, Fiber 1 g, Saturated Fat 0 g, Sodium 2 mg, Sugar 21 g

*Dairy-Free
Açaí Bowl*

Plant-based ice cream can be *even better* than traditional ice cream.

JOY OF BLENDING

Maple Pecan Vegan Ice Cream

MAPLE PECAN VEGAN ICE CREAM

Shared by: JoyofBlending.com, a blog about preparing tasty, healthy food with a powerful blender

  / 5 servings / *Total time:* 3 hours 20 minutes

INGREDIENTS

1⅓ cups (130 g) whole roasted pecans

1½ cups minus 1 Tablespoon (340 ml) water

½ cup (120 ml) maple syrup

¼ teaspoon salt (optional)

INSTRUCTIONS

Place all ingredients into the container in the order listed and secure the lid. Start the Vitamix on its lowest speed, then quickly increase to its highest speed. Blend for 90 seconds.

Pour mixture into an ice cube tray and freeze until solid, at least 3 hours.

Remove the ice cube trays and allow to sit at room temperature for 10 minutes. Place all the cubes into the container and secure the lid. Start the Vitamix on its lowest speed, then quickly increase to its highest speed, using the tamper to press ingredients toward the blades. In about 30–60 seconds, the sound of the motor will change and four mounds should form in the mixture. Stop the Vitamix. Do not overblend or mixture will melt. Serve immediately with more toasted chopped pecans.

Note: If measuring metric weight, water is 340 g and maple syrup is 150 g.

Amount per (127 g) serving: Calories 270, Protein 2 g, Total Fat 19 g, Carbohydrates 25 g, Cholesterol 16 mg, Fiber 2 g, Saturated Fat 2 g, Sodium 180 mg, Sugar 21 g

CASHEW ICE CREAM

Shared by: Vitamix / *Published in:* 1958 at the Pomona Fair

  / 6 servings / *Total time:* 4 hours 20 minutes

INGREDIENTS

1 cup (130 g) whole raw unsalted cashews

1 (13.5-ounce, 400 ml) can coconut milk, or 1¾ cup homemade **Coconut Milk** (see page 175)

¾ cup (180 ml) water

2 Tablespoons cornstarch

½ cup (50 g) pitted dates or honey

INSTRUCTIONS

Place all ingredients into the container in the order listed and secure the lid. Start the Vitamix on its lowest speed, then quickly increase to its highest speed. Blend for 5 minutes 45 seconds or until heavy steam escapes the vented lid.

Pour mixture into ice cube trays and freeze 4 hours or overnight.

Remove the ice cube trays and allow to sit at room temperature for 10 minutes. Place all the cubes into the container and secure the lid. Start the Vitamix on its lowest speed, then quickly increase to its highest speed, using the tamper to press ingredients toward the blades. In about 30–60 seconds, the sound of the motor will change and four mounds should form in the mixture. Stop the Vitamix. Do not overblend or mixture will melt. Serve immediately.

Amount per (131 g) serving: Calories 180, Protein 4 g, Total Fat 11 g, Carbohydrates 17 g, Cholesterol 7 mg, Fiber 1 g, Saturated Fat 3 g, Sodium 20 mg, Sugar 9 g

GREEN LEMON SORBET

Shared by: Terrina Kramer, Vitamix Manager, Territory Sales

  / 8 servings / *Total time:* 10 minutes

INGREDIENTS

2 lemons

½ medium avocado (90 g), pitted and peeled

2 cups (60 g) fresh spinach

⅓ cup (90 ml) **Date Syrup** (see page 176) or honey

3¼ cups (450 g) ice cubes

INSTRUCTIONS

Use a microplane or grater to zest the lemon. With a peeler or paring knife, remove the bitter white pith (optional). Add the zest and fruit to the container.

Place all remaining ingredients into the container in the order listed and secure the lid. Start the Vitamix on its lowest speed, then quickly increase to its highest speed, using the tamper to press ingredients toward the blades. In about 30–60 seconds, the sound of the motor will change and four mounds should form in the mixture. Stop the Vitamix. Do not overblend or mixture will melt. Serve immediately.

Amount per (96 g) serving: Calories 40, Protein 1 g, Total Fat 2 g, Carbohydrates 7 g, Cholesterol 0 mg, Fiber 2 g, Saturated Fat 0 g, Sodium 10 mg, Sugar 4 g

PIÑA COLADA ICE CREAM

Shared by: Cindy Chandler, Vitamix Fan /   / 7 servings / *Total time:* 10 minutes

INGREDIENTS

1 cup (240 ml) **Coconut Milk** (see page 175)

1 medium orange (140 g), peeled

2 cups (260 g) frozen pineapple chunks

1 frozen banana (120 g), peeled and halved

½ cup (30 g) unsweetened shredded coconut

2 dates (30 g), pitted

INSTRUCTIONS

Place all ingredients into the container in the order listed and secure the lid. Start the Vitamix on its lowest speed, then quickly increase to its highest speed, using the tamper to press ingredients toward the blades. In about 30–60 seconds, the sound of the motor will change and four mounds should form in the mixture. Stop the Vitamix. Do not overblend or mixture will melt. Serve immediately.

Amount per (113 g) serving: Calories 150, Protein 2 g, Total Fat 10 g, Carbohydrates 17 g, Cholesterol 12 mg, Fiber 2 g, Saturated Fat 8 g, Sodium 5 mg, Sugar 14 g

"I wouldn't be without my Vitamix! It is the best investment I have ever made in a kitchen appliance."
CINDY CHANDLER

This is a soft serve-style frozen dessert; for a firmer texture, add ½ cup (70g) frozen pineapple.

Green Lemon Sorbet

Chocolate
Chip Caramel
Nice Cream

CHOCOLATE CHIP CARAMEL NICE CREAM

Shared by: Jake McKeon, founder and CEO, Coconut Bowls

48 **64** / 6 servings / *Total time:* 10 minutes

INGREDIENTS

4 frozen bananas (520 g), peeled and halved

4 dates (60 g), pitted

3 Tablespoons (45 g) **Nut Butter** (see page 174) or cashews

1 Tablespoon **Tahini** (see page 97) or sesame seeds

2 teaspoons cocoa powder

¼ cup (30 g) cocoa nibs

Additional cocoa nibs, banana chunks, nut butter, or chopped nuts, for garnish

INSTRUCTIONS

Place all ingredients into the container in the order listed except cocoa nibs and secure the lid. Start the Vitamix on its lowest speed, then quickly increase to its highest speed, using the tamper to press ingredients toward the blades. Blend for 30 seconds using the tamper to press ingredients toward the blades.

Add cocoa nibs. Start the Vitamix on its lowest speed and increase to Variable 4, using the tamper to press ingredients toward the blades. Blend for 5–10 seconds. Serve immediately.

Amount per (113 g) serving: Calories 220, Protein 9 g, Total Fat 12 g, Carbohydrates 23 g, Cholesterol 13 mg, Fiber 5 g, Saturated Fat 3 g, Sodium 30 mg, Sugar 16 g

. . . .

PLANET EARTH'S BEST BANANA NICE CREAM

Shared by: Keegan Allen, actor, photographer, author, and musician

48 **64** / 4 servings / *Total time:* 10 minutes

INGREDIENTS

3 frozen bananas (420 g), peeled and halved

2 Tablespoons **Almond Milk** (see page 175)

1 Tablespoon **Almond Butter** (see page 174)

Add your favorite ice cream mix-ins to the container along with the almond butter: chocolate chips, whole nuts, or coconut.

INSTRUCTIONS

Place bananas and almond milk into the Vitamix container and secure the lid. Select Variable 8. Pulse 15–20 times, using the tamper to press ingredients toward the blades. Add almond butter. Pulse an additional 10 times to incorporate. Serve immediately.

Amount per (116 g) serving: Calories 120, Protein 7 g, Total Fat 3 g, Carbohydrates 18 g, Cholesterol 19 mg, Fiber 3 g, Saturated Fat 0 g, Sodium 15 mg, Sugar 15 g

SWEET SUMMER POPS

Shared by: Euan Mitchell, Vitamix Distributor, Australia

 48 **64** / 8 servings / *Total time:* 8 hours 20 minutes

INGREDIENTS

For the watermelon layer:

2 cups (300 g) watermelon

6 strawberries (150 g)

1 cup (240 ml) **Coconut Milk** (see page 175)

2 teaspoons maple syrup

For the cucumber layer:

1 large cucumber (300 g), peeled

1 cup (240 ml) coconut water

6 fresh mint leaves

3 Tablespoons (45 ml) maple syrup

INSTRUCTIONS

For the watermelon layer: Place the ingredients into the container in the order listed and secure the lid. Start the Vitamix on its lowest speed, then quickly increase to its highest speed, using the tamper to press ingredients toward the blades.

Blend for 30 seconds. Pour mixture into popsicle molds and freeze.

For the cucumber layer: Place the cucumber ingredients into the container and secure the lid. Start the Vitamix on its lowest speed, then quickly increase to its highest speed, using the tamper to press ingredients toward the blades. Blend for 30 seconds. Pour mixture over partially frozen watermelon layer and freeze until solid.

Amount per (82 g) serving: Calories 30, Protein 1 g, Total Fat 0 g, Carbohydrates 7 g, Cholesterol 158 mg, Fiber 1 g, Saturated Fat 0 g, Sodium 10 mg, Sugar 6 g

> It's become a *family summer challenge* to create variable flavors of these pops using local fresh produce! EUAN MITCHELL

CHOCOLATE PUDDING

Shared by: Vitamix / *Published in:* 1975 / **48** **64** / 10 servings / *Total time:* 40 minutes

INGREDIENTS

4 cups (960 ml) **Almond Milk** (see page 175)

½ cup (60 g) pitted dates or alternative sweetener

1 large egg

¼ cup (25 g) unsweetened cocoa powder

6 Tablespoons (50 g) cornstarch

INSTRUCTIONS

Place all ingredients into the container in the order listed and secure the lid. Start the Vitamix on its lowest speed, then quickly increase to its highest speed. Blend for 5 minutes 45 seconds or until heavy steam escapes the lid plug. Let cool before serving.

Amount per (123 g) serving: Calories 17, Protein 0 g, Total Fat 0 g, Carbohydrates 4 g, Cholesterol 4 mg, Fiber 0 g, Saturated Fat 0 g, Sodium 0 mg, Sugar 0 g

Sweet Summer Pops

*Brownie
Truffles*

BROWNIE TRUFFLES

Shared by: Sean Bowyer, Vitamix Fan / **64** Low Profile / 18 servings / *Total time:* 10 minutes

INGREDIENTS

2 cups (280 g) whole roasted unsalted almonds

1 cup (100 g) cocoa powder

½ cup (65 g) dried cranberries

½ cup (90 g) flax seed

Flaked coconut, Matcha powder, cocoa powder, or finely chopped nuts, for finishing

INSTRUCTIONS

Place all ingredients in the container in the order listed and secure the lid. Start the Vitamix on its lowest speed, then quickly increase to its highest speed, using the tamper to press ingredients toward the blades. Blend for 45 seconds.

Scoop out about 2 Tablespoons of mixture and shape into a ball; repeat with remaining mixture. Roll each truffle in your favorite topping.

Amount per (33 g) serving: Calories 170, Protein 5 g, Total Fat 12 g, Carbohydrates 13 g, Cholesterol 3 mg, Fiber 3 g, Saturated Fat 2 g, Sodium 35 mg, Sugar 6 g

FRUIT SCROLLS

Shared by: Suzanne Gagne, Vitamix Demonstrator, Canada / **64** / 20 servings / *Total time:* 10 hours

INGREDIENTS

2 cups (480 ml) water

3 cups (375 g) fresh or frozen mixed berries

2 Tablespoons chia seed

3 cups (90 g) fresh spinach or kale

5 dates (75 g), pitted

1½ lemons, peeled

½ medium beet (50 g), washed

2 Tablespoons honey (optional)

1 Tablespoon maple syrup (optional)

INSTRUCTIONS

Place all ingredients into the container in the order listed and secure the lid. Start the Vitamix on its lowest speed, then quickly increase to its highest speed, using the tamper to press ingredients toward the blades. Blend for 1 minute.

Spread mixture on dehydrator sheets and dehydrate at 155°F (68°C) for 1 hour, lower to 105°F (40°C) for 6–8 hours or until no longer sticky. (Alternately, spread the mixture onto a parchment-lined baking sheet and bake in the oven at its lowest temperature with oven door slightly open, until no longer sticky.) Cut with a pizza cutter into long strips and roll up. Let cool. Store in an airtight container in a cool, dry area.

Amount per (27 g) serving: Calories 25, Protein 1 g, Total Fat 0 g, Carbohydrates 6 g, Cholesterol 0 mg, Fiber 2 g, Saturated Fat 0 g, Sodium 5 mg, Sugar 4 g

> "Vitamix has changed my life because it allows me to get a lot more nutrition into my diet than I otherwise could. The Vitamix makes eating healthy quick and easy."
> SUZANNE GAGNE

NO-BAKE VEGAN CHEESECAKE

Shared by: Leeyel Diamond, Vitamix Fan / **64** Low Profile / 10 servings / *Total time:* 3 hours 30 minutes

INGREDIENTS

For the crust:

½ cup (70 g) whole roasted unsalted almonds

½ cup (60 g) gluten-free rolled oats

2 Tablespoons flax seed

2 Tablespoons chia seed

2 Tablespoons hemp seed

Pinch of Himalayan pink salt (optional)

1 cup (140 g) Medjool dates, pitted

2 teaspoons spirulina (optional)

For the filling:

1½ cups (205 g) whole raw cashews, soaked overnight in water to cover and drained

⅔ cup (180 ml) **Coconut Milk** (see page 175)

⅓ cup (90 ml) coconut oil

⅓ cup (90 ml) maple syrup

1 lemon, peeled, or ⅓ cup (90 ml) fresh lemon juice

1 teaspoon vanilla extract

INSTRUCTIONS

For the crust: Place all ingredients except the dates into the container in the order listed and secure the lid. Start the Vitamix on its lowest speed, then quickly increase to Variable 6. Blend for 20 seconds until mixture is crumbled. Add the dates and blend on Variable 5 for 15 seconds, using the tamper to press ingredients toward the blades, until well processed.

Line a 9-inch pie pan with a round of parchment. Transfer crust mixture to the pan and press firmly into bottom and up sides of pan. Place in the freezer while you prepare the filling.

For the filling: Place all ingredients into the container in the order listed and secure the lid. Start the Vitamix on its lowest speed, then quickly increase to its highest speed. Blend for 45 seconds or until smooth. Pour filling into crust.

Place pan in the freezer for 3 hours or until firm. When you are ready to serve, let the cheesecake thaw for 15 minutes before slicing.

Amount per (106 g) serving: Calories 370, Protein 8 g, Total Fat 23 g, Carbohydrates 34 g, Cholesterol 16 mg, Fiber 5 g, Saturated Fat 9 g, Sodium 40 mg, Sugar 20 g

> " Since I got my Vitamix, my consumption of vegetables has *skyrocketed* and made the transition of going more plant-based simple. I love all of the possibilities. LEEYEL DIAMOND

*Chocolate
Avocado
Pudding*

CHOCOLATE AVOCADO PUDDING

Shared by: Vitamix / *Published in:* 2000 /   / 8 servings / *Total time:* 10 minutes

INGREDIENTS

2 avocados (415 g), halved, pitted, and peeled

⅔ cup (160 ml) **Almond Milk** (see page 175)

½ cup (50 g) pitted dates or maple syrup

¼ cup (20 g) cocoa powder

When using the 64-ounce Low-Profile container, double the recipe for best results.

INSTRUCTIONS

Place all ingredients into the container in the order listed and secure the lid. Start the Vitamix on its lowest speed, then quickly increase to its highest speed, using the tamper to press ingredients toward the blades. Blend for 30–45 seconds or until desired consistency is reached.

Amount per (81 g) serving: Calories 100, Protein 1 g, Total Fat 8 g, Carbohydrates 9 g, Cholesterol 4 mg, Fiber 4 g, Saturated Fat 0 g, Sodium 4 mg, Sugar 1 g

CHERRY OATMEAL BITES

Shared by: Leslie Tauro, Vitamix Fan / / 20 servings / *Total time:* 50 minutes

INGREDIENTS

1½ cups (205 g) whole roasted unsalted cashews, soaked in water to cover for 10 minutes and drained

¼ cup (80 g) **Date Syrup** (see page 176) or pomegranate molasses

5 Medjool dates (80 g), pitted

1 cup (140 g) whole roasted unsalted almonds

2 cups (160 g) rolled oats

1 cup (60 g) dried cherries

INSTRUCTIONS

Place drained cashews, date syrup, and dates into the container and secure the lid. Start the Vitamix on its lowest speed, then quickly increase to its highest speed, using the tamper to press ingredients toward the blades. Blend until a smooth paste forms.

Add the almonds and oats. Select Variable 7. Pulse 20–25 times until processed, using the tamper to press ingredients toward the blades. There will still be texture to the oats and almonds. Remove the mixture to a bowl and stir in the cherries.

Roll into two logs about ½ inch (1.25 cm) in diameter and wrap in plastic. Refrigerate for 30 minutes. Slice into ½-inch (1.25 cm) thick rounds. Store bites in an airtight container in the refrigerator.

Amount per (36 g) serving: Calories 160, Protein 5 g, Total Fat 9 g, Carbohydrates 17 g, Cholesterol 3 mg, Fiber 2 g, Saturated Fat 1 g, Sodium 2 mg, Sugar 8 g

HOT CHOCOLATE SAUCE

Shared by: Marta Villen, Vitamix Distributor, Spain / **64** / 48 servings / *Total time:* 10 minutes

INGREDIENTS

4 cups (960 ml) water

½ cup (50 g) rolled oats

1 cup (100 g) unsweetened cocoa powder

⅓ cup (50 g) cornstarch

⅔ cup (150 ml) maple syrup or **Date Syrup** (see page 176)

1 teaspoon ground cinnamon

INSTRUCTIONS

Place all ingredients into the container in the order listed and secure the lid. Start the Vitamix on its lowest speed, then quickly increase to its highest speed. Blend for 5 minutes 45 seconds.

Amount per (28 g) serving: Calories 25, Protein 1 g, Total Fat 0 g, Carbohydrates 6 g, Cholesterol 2 mg, Fiber 1 g, Saturated Fat 0 g, Sodium 1 mg, Sugar 3 g

BERRY FROZEN YOGURT

Shared by: Kristie Jarrett, Vitamix Senior Program Manager, Engineering
  / 8 servings / *Total time:* 10 minutes

INGREDIENTS

1 cup (240 ml) non-dairy yogurt or vanilla yogurt

2 cups (260 g) frozen strawberries

1 cup (120 g) frozen blueberries

½ cup (60 g) frozen raspberries

½ medium frozen banana (50 g), peeled

1½ cups (45 g) fresh spinach

1 small carrot (50 g)

INSTRUCTIONS

Place all ingredients into the container in the order listed and secure the lid. Start the Vitamix on its lowest speed, then quickly increase to its highest speed using the tamper to press ingredients toward the blades. In about 30–60 seconds, the sound of the motor will change and four mounds should form in the mixture. Stop the Vitamix. Do not overblend or mixture will melt. Serve immediately.

Amount per (104 g) serving: Calories 60, Protein 2 g, Total Fat 0 g, Carbohydrates 12 g, Cholesterol 4 mg, Fiber 1 g, Saturated Fat 0 g, Sodium 30 mg, Sugar 9 g

> "This is my family's all-time favorite. I didn't let my kids see what I was putting into it so they couldn't turn up their noses."
> KRISTIE JARRETT

This frozen dessert can easily be turned into a smoothie by adding 1½ cups water.

*Hot Chocolate
Sauce*

Pure & Simple

Commercial baby foods are highly processed and often contain preservatives. Homemade baby food is pure and natural.

Make & Freeze

All kinds of blended foods can be made in big batches, portioned into single-serving containers or ice cube trays, and frozen. Reheat carefully; be sure to test temperature before feeding.

Mix It Up!

Babies have undeveloped palates and respond best to simple flavors—but that doesn't mean boring. Mix and match unseasoned whole foods to develop your little one's expanding palate.

Get Expert Guidance

Always consult with your pediatrician to get the right guidance on what and how to feed your growing baby.

Add Fiber

Brown rice adds a little fiber and whole grain to your baby's diet. A blend of steamed tomatoes and brown rice makes a savory combination that's filling and easily digestible.

BABY FOODS

My grandparents Bill and Ruth recognized that whole foods were the best way to start their six children on the journey to health and wellness. I recall watching my Grandpa Bill grind whole wheat berries and knead bread in the Vitamix in under 3 minutes; while the loaf was baking Grandma Ruth used it to make fresh Raw Applesauce (see page 95) to spread on top. They knew that whole foods were full of nutrients that little bodies needed in order to develop physically and mentally. What they did not know at the time was that the food we feed our children, starting with puréed foods, has an impact on that child's food choices and preferences for the rest of their life.

> **I show love with food, so *I felt good* feeding my daughters blends that I prepared myself, organic and free of preservatives.** JEN PICCIANO

Think about this: We can influence the health and wellness, as well as the food preferences, of the children in our lives for generations to come. Your choices today may have an impact on your descendants 100 years from now.

We now know that introducing a range of flavors expands your child's exposure to new foods—and since they have not learned what foods *not* to like, you can load them up with superfoods! Experiment with our Mix & Match Purée recipe (see facing page).

Not only can you whip up foods your infant will love, but it's super quick and easy to create smooth purées or chunkier textures as your child gets older. If you make a big batch, divide it into single-serving containers and freeze for easy prep later, or even set aside a portion of your family dinner to blend into an easy-to-feed meal for your toddler.

Food for your infant needs to be very smooth; for this reason, parents are sometimes discouraged from blending raw food in most blenders. The Vitamix is a power horse that will create a smooth purée out of just about anything—making more raw foods an option. That does not mean every food is appropriate; always consult your pediatrician for guidance on whether or not raw or cooked ingredients are right for your child. Research suggests that plant-based, whole-food nutrition is beneficial from an early age to set your child up for a lifetime of good health (learn more about our efforts with the Vitamix Foundation at 100.Vitamix.com/1st2000).

My Grandma Ruth would be proud to know that you chose to nurture your little one with fresh, wholesome food!

MIX & MATCH PURÉE

Shared by: Vitamix / *Published in:* 1999 / **32** **48** **64** / *Total time:* 10 minutes

INGREDIENTS

Fruit options (peeled and seeded as needed):
banana, peach, avocado, papaya, mango, apple, pear

Vegetable options (peeled and seeded as needed):
sweet potato, peas, squash, carrot, green beans, spinach, corn

INSTRUCTIONS

Choose one or more options from the list at left. Place 2 cups (300 g) of fruits and/or vegetables into the container along with ¼ cup (60 ml) water, formula, or breast milk and secure the lid. Start the Vitamix on its lowest speed, then quickly increase to its highest speed, using the tamper to press ingredients toward the blades. Blend for 1 minute or until desired consistency is reached.

Store in an airtight container in the refrigerator for up to 3 days.

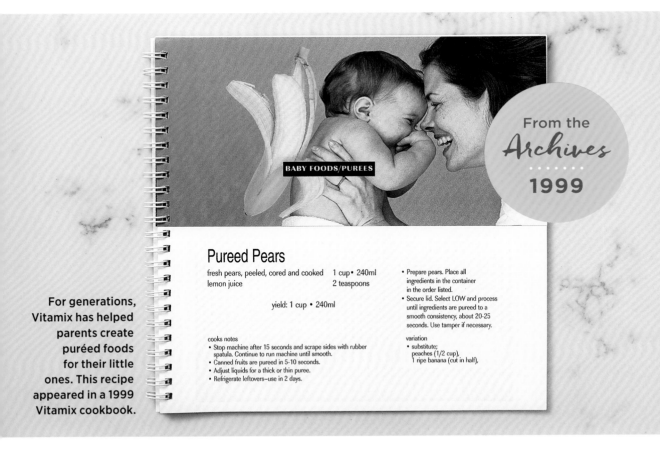

BABY FOODS/PUREES

From the *Archives* 1999

For generations, Vitamix has helped parents create puréed foods for their little ones. This recipe appeared in a 1999 Vitamix cookbook.

Pureed Pears

fresh pears, peeled, cored and cooked	1 cup • 240ml
lemon juice	2 teaspoons

yield: 1 cup • 240ml

cooks notes
- Stop machine after 15 seconds and scrape sides with rubber spatula. Continue to run machine until smooth.
- Canned fruits are pureed in 5-10 seconds.
- Adjust liquids for a thick or thin puree.
- Refrigerate leftovers–use in 2 days.

- Prepare pears. Place all ingredients in the container in the order listed.
- Secure lid. Select LOW and process until ingredients are pureed to a smooth consistency, about 20-25 seconds. Use tamper if necessary.

variation
- substitute;
  peaches (1/2 cup),
  1 ripe banana (cut in half),

APPLE & PUMPKIN BABY FOOD

Shared by: Laura Sandford, mom, cook, photographer, and blogger at JoyFoodSunshine.com

 32 **48** **64** / 20 servings / *Total time:* 10 minutes

INGREDIENTS

1 small pie pumpkin (250 g), roasted until tender (about 1½ cups cooked pumpkin)

3 medium apples (410 g), halved and cored

INSTRUCTIONS

Place pumpkin and apples into the container and secure the lid. Start the Vitamix on its lowest speed, then quickly increase to its highest speed.

Blend for 1 minute. If necessary, add up to ½ cup water and continue blending until mixture reaches desired consistency. (Younger babies [4–7 months] need a thinner purée, while older babies [8+ months] can handle a little bit of texture.)

Amount per (31 g) serving: Calories 15, Protein 0 g, Total Fat 0 g, Carbohydrates 4 g, Cholesterol 2 mg, Fiber 1 g, Saturated Fat 0 g, Sodium 0 mg, Sugar 3 g

SUPER PORRIDGE BABY FOOD

Shared by: Christine Carlson, Vitamix Program Manager, New Product Development

 32 **48** / 40 servings / *Total time:* 15 minutes

INGREDIENTS

¼ cup (50 g) brown rice

¼ cup (55 g) millet

¼ cup (20 g) rolled oats

3 cups (720 ml) water

INSTRUCTIONS

Place rice, millet, and oats into the container and secure the lid. Start the Vitamix on its lowest speed, then quickly increase to its highest speed. Blend for 1 minute.

Place water in a saucepan and bring to a boil. Sprinkle grain over boiling water and whisk briskly. Cover and cook on low for about 10 minutes, whisking frequently to prevent scorching.

Let cool completely, then store in an airtight container in the refrigerator for up to 3 days.

Adapted from Super Baby Food *by Ruth Yarron*

Amount per (28 g) serving: Calories 10, Protein 0 g, Total Fat 0 g, Carbohydrates 2 g, Cholesterol 0 mg, Fiber 0 g, Saturated Fat 0 g, Sodium 0 mg, Sugar 0 g

Apple & Pumpkin Baby Food

Protein-Packed Purée

> **Vitamix** *empowered me* **as a new mom. Its power, user-friendly features, and self-cleaning mode made it easy for me to prepare homemade baby food for all three of my daughters.** JEN PICCIANO

PROTEIN-PACKED PURÉE

Shared by: Jen Picciano, reporter for WOIO-TV and creator of the food segment "Cleveland Cooks"

  / 12 servings / *Total time:* 10 minutes

INGREDIENTS

1 (15-ounce, 425 g) can chickpeas, drained, liquid reserved

1 baked sweet potato (140 g), skin on

INSTRUCTIONS

Place chickpeas, chickpea liquid, and sweet potato into the container and secure the lid. Start the Vitamix on its lowest speed, then quickly increase to its highest speed, using the tamper to press ingredients toward the blades. Blend for 1 minute or until desired consistency is reached.

Amount per (31 g) serving: Calories 40, Protein 2 g, Total Fat 1 g, Carbohydrates 7 g, Cholesterol 1 mg, Fiber 2 g, Saturated Fat 0 g, Sodium 50 mg, Sugar 1 g

PEAR-PRUNE PURÉE

Shared by: Christine Carlson, Vitamix Program Manager, New Product Development

  / 50 servings / *Total time:* 25 minutes

INGREDIENTS

6 large pears (720 g), cored and halved

1 cup (140 g) pitted prunes

1½ cups (360 ml) water

INSTRUCTIONS

Combine all ingredients in a saucepan and bring to a simmer; cook until pears and prunes are tender, 10–20 minutes.

Place ingredients into the container in the order listed and secure the lid. Start the Vitamix on its lowest speed, then quickly increase to its highest speed. Blend for 30–60 seconds or until desired consistency is reached.

Amount per (31 g) serving: Calories 20, Protein 0 g, Total Fat 0 g, Carbohydrates 5 g, Cholesterol 4 mg, Fiber 1 g, Saturated Fat 0 g, Sodium 0 mg, Sugar 3 g

Ask Your Vet

Before altering your pet's diet, check with your veterinarian to be sure you're meeting the animal's nutritional needs.

Vitamix Variety

Your Vitamix allows you to blend up healthy fresh, baked, or frozen treats for your pets. You'll save money and use ingredients you trust.

Just a Treat

The recipes included here are not meant to substitute for your pet's regular food, but rather for occasional treats.

PET TREATS

Did you know that Americans spend nearly $73 billion a year on our four-legged family members?

As the amount of money we spend and the body of science that connects the dots between human health and diet grows, we've also come to understand that our pet's wellness depends on what we put into their food bowls. After all, our pets rely on us to keep them healthy and safe, and it's never been easier to take control of their nutrition. Whipping up easy treats in your Vitamix using ingredients you know and trust means that you can show your love while managing your budget.

> "If you are like me, your pets are part of your family, and making *healthier choices* for yourself and them is easy with the Vitamix. CINDY RYBARCZYK

Just like you, our employees dote on their dogs and cats (and the occasional horse and rabbit). Several of the recipes here are shared by Vitamix employee Cindy Rybarczyk, who loves making homemade treats for her dogs and who helped create a booklet of Vitamix recipes for pets back in 2011 (see facing page). Cindy's mother, Alice, was also a longtime Vitamix employee. When we say that Vitamix is a family business, it's not just *our* family; it's also generations of other families who've worked alongside us for so many years.

Why pay for fancy packaging and artificial flavors when you can make your own pet treats with ingredients you trust and love? Your pets will be on their best behavior!

Grandpa Bill had joyful, laughing eyes and a fondness for the family's pets.

Pet Treats

All-natural, homemade Vitamix Treats...

are perfect for everyone in the family, including your pets. Fresh from the Vitamix test kitchen, these easy-to-make recipes are not part of any special pet diet, but are veterinarian-approved for pet safety. Instead of paying for packaging, additives and preservatives, make these healthy pet treats, with natural ingredients and love, in your Vitamix. Your pets will be begging for more!

Vitamix.

We love our pets so much that our team created this booklet of treats made with whole ingredients and lots of love.

PUMPKIN CAT FOOD TOPPER

Shared by: Vitamix / *Published in:* 2011 / **48** **64** / Varies / *Total time:* 10 minutes

INGREDIENTS

¾ cup (180 ml) water

1 cup (245 g) cooked pumpkin

¼ cup (35 g) unsalted pumpkin seeds

1 (6 ounce, 170 gram) can chunk light tuna in water

INSTRUCTIONS

Place all ingredients into the container in the order listed and secure the lid. Start the Vitamix on its lowest speed and increase to its highest speed, using the tamper to press ingredients toward the blades. Blend for 30–45 seconds or until smooth.

FROSTY STRAWBERRY DOG TREATS

Shared by: Cindy Rybarczyk, Vitamix Senior Graphic Designer

  64 Classic / 12 servings / *Total time:* 10 minutes

INGREDIENTS

1 cup (150 g) frozen strawberries

¾ cup (180 ml) plain yogurt

INSTRUCTIONS

Place ingredients into the container and secure the lid. Start the Vitamix on its lowest speed, then quickly increase to its highest speed, using the tamper to press ingredients toward the blades. Blend for 45 seconds. Pour into ice cube tray and freeze solid. Pop out frozen treats and store in a resealable plastic bag in the freezer.

LIVER TREATS

Shared by: Cindy Rybarczyk, Vitamix Senior Graphic Designer

  / 20 servings / *Total time:* 20 minutes

INGREDIENTS

2 cups (160 g) old-fashioned rolled oats

¼ pound (110 g) raw beef or chicken liver

1 large egg

2 Tablespoons honey

3 Tablespoons (45 ml) olive oil

INSTRUCTIONS

Preheat oven to 350°F (180°C).

Place oats into the container and secure the lid. Start the Vitamix on its lowest speed, then quickly increase to its highest speed. Blend for 30 seconds; transfer oats to a large bowl.

Place the remaining ingredients into the container and secure lid. Start the Vitamix on its lowest speed, then quickly increase to its highest speed, using the tamper to press ingredients toward the blades. Blend for 30 seconds. Add to ground oats and mix to create a dough.

OPTIONS FOR BAKING:

For shapes: Let the dough rest for 10–15 minutes to stiffen. Roll the dough out on a floured surface to ¼ inch (.6 cm) thickness. Cut into desired shapes with cookie cutters, rerolling scraps as needed. Transfer to a lightly greased baking sheet. Bake for 8–12 minutes, until biscuits are firm and lightly browned.

For kisses: Transfer dough to a plastic bag; snip about ½ inch off one corner of the bag. Pipe "kisses" onto a lightly greased baking pan. (Alternately, drop dough by teaspoonfuls onto baking sheet.) Bake for 8–10 minutes or until lightly golden.

For chewy bites: Press the dough into a greased 8-inch (20 cm) square baking pan. Bake for 15–20 minutes. Let cool; remove from pan and cut into small "bites."

Store chewy versions of these treats in the refrigerator or freezer.

Frosty Strawberry Dog Treats

Simple Dog Biscuits →

SIMPLE DOG BISCUITS

Shared by: Vitamix / *Published in:* 2011 / **64** / 10 biscuits / *Total time:* 50 minutes

INGREDIENTS

1⅓ cups (220 ml) **Peanut Butter** (see page 174)

1¼ cups (300 ml) hot water

2 cups (240 g) **Whole Wheat Flour** (see page 177)

1 cup (80 cups) old-fashioned rolled oats

INSTRUCTIONS

Preheat oven to 350°F (180°C); line a baking sheet with parchment.

Place the peanut butter and hot water into the container and secure the lid. Start the Vitamix on its lowest speed, then quickly increase to its highest speed, using the tamper to press ingredients toward the blades. Blend for 30 seconds. Remove lid and add flour and oats. Secure the lid and select Variable 6. Pulse 5–6 times. You will notice the dough starting to form a ball and lift off the blades. Remove the lid and scrape down the sides, adding a little flour if the dough looks too moist and has not formed a ball. Pulse again 5–6 times.

Transfer dough onto a floured work surface and knead for 1–2 minutes. Roll out dough to ¼ inch (.6 cm) thickness and use your favorite cookie cutter to cut into shapes. Bake for about 40 minutes, or until thoroughly dry. Transfer biscuits to a wire rack to cool completely.

DOG KIBBLE TOPPER

Shared by: James Orth, Vitamix Fan / **48** **64** / Varies / *Total time:* 20 minutes

INGREDIENTS

4 chicken leg quarters

2 sweet potatoes, peeled and quartered

INSTRUCTIONS

Place chicken and potatoes in a pressure cooker; add water to cover. Cook on high for 10 minutes. Transfer chicken and potatoes to a platter and reserve the cooking liquid; let cool.

Place half the chicken and potatoes, and half the cooking liquid into the container and secure the lid. Start the Vitamix on its lowest speed, then quickly increase to its highest speed, using the tamper to press ingredients toward the blades. Blend for 3 minutes or until smooth. Transfer to a bowl, then repeat with remaining chicken, potatoes, and cooking liquid.

Store in an airtight container in the refrigerator for up to 1 week. Spoon the topper over your dog's dry kibble.

Perk up your dog's dry food with a tablespoon or two of this "gravy."

VITAMIX ESSENTIALS

Rely on these basic recipes for everyday staples.

ALMOND BUTTER

48 **64** / 16 servings / *Total time:* 5 minutes

4 cups (600 g) whole roasted unsalted almonds

Place nuts into the container and secure the lid. Start the Vitamix on its lowest speed, then quickly increase to its highest speed, using the tamper to press ingredients toward the blades. In 1 minute, you will hear a high-pitched chugging sound. Continue using the tamper until the almond butter begins to flow freely through the blades. Stop the Vitamix when the sound of the motor changes and becomes low and laboring.

Amount per (35 g) serving: Calories 210, Protein 7 g, Total Fat 18 g, Carbohydrates 7 g, Cholesterol mg, Fiber 4 g, Saturated Fat 2 g, Sodium 0 mg, Sugar 2 g

PEANUT BUTTER

64 / 24 servings / *Total time:* 5 minutes

4 cups (600 g) roasted unsalted peanuts

Place nuts into the container and secure the lid. Start the Vitamix on its lowest speed, then quickly increase to its highest speed, using the tamper to press ingredients toward the blades. In 1 minute, you will hear a high-pitched chugging sound. Continue using the tamper until the peanut butter begins to flow freely through the blades. Stop the Vitamix when the sound of the motor changes and becomes low and laboring or the mixture has reached the desired consistency.

Amount per (247 g) serving: Calories 180, Protein 7 g, Total Fat 15 g, Carbohydrates 6 g, Cholesterol 1 mg, Fiber 3 g, Saturated Fat 3 g, Sodium 2 mg, Sugar 1 g

PEANUT CASHEW BUTTER

48 **64** / 14 servings / *Total time:* 5 minutes

1½ cups (220 g) whole roasted unsalted peanuts

1½ cups (205 g) whole roasted unsalted cashews

Place nuts into the container and secure the lid. Start the Vitamix on its lowest speed, then quickly increase to its highest speed, using the tamper to press ingredients toward the blades. In 1 minute, you will hear a high-pitched chugging sound. Continue using the tamper until the nut butter begins to flow freely through the blades. Stop the Vitamix when the sound of the motor changes and becomes low and laboring.

Store in an airtight container in the refrigerator for maximum shelf life.

Amount per (30 g) serving: Calories 180, Protein 6 g, Total Fat 15 g, Carbohydrates 8 g, Cholesterol 0 mg, Fiber 2 g, Saturated Fat 3 g, Sodium 0 mg, Sugar 2 g

CASHEW CREAM

48 **64** / 20 servings / *Total time:* 2 hours

2 cups (275 g) whole unsalted cashews

1 cup (240 ml) water, plus extra for soaking

Place cashews in a bowl and cover with water. Soak for 2 hours. Rinse and drain the cashews.

Place 1 cup of fresh water and the soaked cashews into the container and secure the lid. Start the Vitamix on its lowest speed, then quickly increase to its highest speed. Blend for 45 seconds, using the tamper as needed to push the ingredients toward the blades.

Amount per (29 g) serving: Calories 80, Protein 2 g, Total Fat 6 g, Carbohydrates 4 g, Cholesterol 1 mg, Fiber 0 g, Saturated Fat 1 g, Sodium 2 mg, Sugar 1 g

ALMOND MILK

48 **64** / 4 servings / *Total time:* 5 minutes

3 cups (720 ml) water

1 cup (140 g) whole raw unsalted almonds

2 dates (30 g), pitted, or other natural sweetener to taste

Few drops vanilla extract, to taste (optional)

Place all ingredients into the container in the order listed and secure the lid. Start the Vitamix on its lowest speed, then quickly increase to its highest speed. Blend for 1 minute or until desired consistency is reached.

Store in an airtight container in the refrigerator; shake well before using.

Note: If desired, soak almonds in cold water for 4 hours or overnight, then drain. You can easily double this recipe in the 64-ounce container.

Amount per (221 g) serving: Calories 230, Protein 8 g, Total Fat 18 g, Carbohydrates 13 g, Cholesterol mg, Fiber 5 g, Saturated Fat 2 g, Sodium 10 mg, Sugar 7 g

COCONUT MILK

64 / 4.5 servings / *Total time:* 5 minutes

4 cups (960 ml) water

2 cups (150 g) unsweetened shredded coconut

Place all ingredients into the container in the order listed and secure the lid. Start the Vitamix on its lowest speed, then quickly increase to its highest speed. Blend for 1 minute or until desired consistency is reached.

Store in an airtight container in the refrigerator; shake well before using.

Amount per (247 g) serving: Calories 240, Protein 2 g, Total Fat 21 g, Carbohydrates 9 g, Cholesterol 2 mg, Fiber 7 g, Saturated Fat 19 g, Sodium 10 mg, Sugar 2 g

OAT MILK

64 / 6 servings / *Total time:* 4 hours

½ cup (90 g) steel-cut oats, soaked for 4 hours, drained, and rinsed

6 cups (1.2 l) cold water

Place the oats and water into the container and secure the lid. Start the Vitamix on its lowest speed, then quickly increase to its highest speed. Blend for 30–45 seconds. Remove and strain through a fine mesh strainer.

Store in an airtight container in the refrigerator; shake well before using.

Note: You can customize the taste of this dairy-free milk by adding pitted dates, vanilla extract, salt—or all three—to taste.

Amount per (262 g) serving: Calories 60, Protein 2 g, Total Fat 1 g, Carbohydrates 10 g, Cholesterol 0 mg, Fiber 2 g, Saturated Fat 0 g, Sodium 10 mg, Sugar 0 g

SOY MILK

48 **64** / 4 servings
Total time: 4 hours, 30 minutes

1 cup (200 g) dried soybeans

2 dates (30 g), pitted, or other natural sweetener to taste

4 cups (960 ml) water

Rinse soybeans and soak in water for 4–8 hours. Drain, then transfer to a steamer basket set over a pan of simmering water and team for 15 minutes or until tender. Drain and cool. Measure 1½ cups (260 g) of cooked beans.

Place cooked beans, dates, and water into the container in the order listed and secure the lid. Start the Vitamix on its lowest speed, then quickly increase to its highest speed. Blend for 45 seconds or until desired consistency is reached.

Store in an airtight container in the refrigerator.

Note: For a commercial-style soy milk, strain the liquid through a filtration bag or fine mesh sieve. For a refreshing flavor, add a 1-inch (2.5 cm) slice of fresh ginger root before blending.

Amount per (294 g) serving: Calories 100, Protein 9 g, Total Fat 5 g, Carbohydrates 7 g, Cholesterol 0 mg, Fiber 3 g, Saturated Fat 1 g, Sodium 10 mg, Sugar 4 g

DATE SYRUP

20 / 10 servings / *Total time:* 35 minutes

¾ cup (130 g) pitted dates

1½ cups (360 ml) hot water

Steep dates in water for 30 minutes. Place dates and water into the container and secure the blade base.

Start the Vitamix on its lowest speed, then quickly increase to its highest speed. Blend for 1 minute.

Note: If using a larger Vitamix container, you can double or triple the recipe. Use in place of honey or other sweeteners or reduce over medium heat to create a thicker syrup for pancakes or cocktails.

Amount per (37 g) serving: Calories 35, Protein 0 g, Total Fat 0 g, Carbohydrates 9 g, Cholesterol 9 mg, Fiber 1 g, Saturated Fat 0 g, Sodium 0 mg, Sugar 8 g

ORANGE JUICE

64 / 2 servings / *Total time:* 5 minutes

½ cup (120 ml) water

4 dates (30 g), pitted, or 2 Tablespoons honey

4 medium oranges (600 g), peeled

1½ cups (200 g) ice cubes

Place all ingredients into the container in the order listed and secure lid. Start the Vitamix on its lowest speed, then quickly increase to its highest speed, using the tamper to press ingredients toward the blades. Blend for 1 minute or until desired consistency is reached.

Amount per (452 g) serving: Calories 190, Protein 3 g, Total Fat 0 g, Carbohydrates 48 g, Cholesterol mg, Fiber 6 g, Saturated Fat 0 g, Sodium 10 mg, Sugar 37 g

CORNMEAL

64 / 5 servings / *Total time:* 5 minutes

3 cups (500 g) unpopped popcorn kernels

Place kernels into the container and secure the lid. Start the Vitamix on its lowest speed, then quickly increase to its highest speed. Process for 30–60 seconds or until desired consistency is reached.

Note: Grits and polenta have a coarser grind than cornmeal used for baking.

Amount per (100 g) serving: Calories 380, Protein 11 g, Total Fat 5 g, Carbohydrates 74 g, Cholesterol 0 mg, Fiber 13 g, Saturated Fat 1 g, Sodium 5 mg, Sugar 1 g

WHOLE WHEAT FLOUR

32 **48** **64** / 4 servings / *Total time:* 5 minutes

2 cups (375 g) whole wheat kernels

Place whole wheat kernels into the container and secure the lid. Start the Vitamix on its lowest speed, then quickly increase to its highest speed. Grind to desired degree of fineness. The longer the Vitamix runs, the finer the consistency of the flour, around 1 minute on highest speed for very fine whole wheat flour. Sift after blending if desired. See Grain Grinding chart on page 30.

Amount per (94 g) serving: Calories 320, Protein 12 g, Total Fat 2 g, Carbohydrates 68 g, Cholesterol 0 mg, Fiber 14 g, Saturated Fat 0 g, Sodium 0 mg, Sugar 0 g

RECIPE INDEX

AFFILIATES & DISTRIBUTORS

Avocado Soup
Shared by: Mads Bo 124

Creamy Wild Rice Soup
Shared by: Shalva and Lenny Gale 120

Herb-Infused Creamy Sweet Onion Soup
Shared by: Dan Henry Parker Jr. 115

Hot Chocolate Sauce
Shared by: Marta Villen 156

Hummus
Shared by: Mira Gil 70

Maple Pecan Vegan Ice Cream
Shared by: JoyofBlending.com 143

Matbukha
Shared by: Chen Assor 73

Raspberry Dijon Dressing
Shared by: Randall Weiss 90

Sweet Summer Pops
Shared by: Euan Mitchell 148

CELEBRITIES & INFLUENCERS

Apple & Pumpkin Baby Food
Shared by: Laura Sandford 162

Carrot Ginger Soup
Shared by: Jen Picciano 119

Chocolate Chip Caramel Nice Cream
Shared by: Jake McKeon 147

Creamy Broccoli Soup
Shared by: Alison Wu 123

Green Goddess Hummus
Shared by: Lisa Bryan 70

Mango Turmeric Smoothie
Shared by: Danny Seo 47

mindbodygreen Smoothie
Shared by: Colleen and Jason Wachob 51

Non-Dairy Caesar Dressing & Salad
Shared by: Marilu Henner 90

Nutritarian Caesar Dressing
Shared by: Dr. Joel Fuhrman 89

Orange Sesame Dressing
Shared by: Dr. Joel Fuhrman 89

Planet Earth's Best Banana Nice Cream
Shared by: Keegan Allen 147

Protein-Packed Purée
Shared by: Jen Picciano 165

Spa Smoothie
Shared by: Kelly LeVeque 43

Ultra-Creamy Cashew Butter Coffee
Shared by: Dr. Mark Hyman 63

Vietnamese Dressing
Shared by: Bobby Berk 86

CHEFS & BARTENDERS

Fra Diavolo Sauce
Shared by: Chris Cosentino 109

Hearts of Palm Ceviche
Shared by: Alejandra Schrader 106

Sesame Zucchini with
Parmesan Basil Ganache
Shared by: Jehangir Mehta 108

Spotted Owl Piña Colada
Shared by: Will Hollingsworth 56

FROM THE VITAMIX ARCHIVES

Applesauce Cookies 132

Cashew Ice Cream 143

Chocolate Avocado Pudding 155

Chocolate Pudding 148

Citrus Sangria 55

Classic Vitamix Rainbow Smoothie 47

Grandpa's Pancakes 132

Lime Mint Agua Fresca 59

Mix & Match Purée 161

Pumpkin Cat Food Topper 169

Raw Applesauce 95

Sesame Dressing 86

Simple Dog Biscuits 173

Soft Ginger Cookies 131

Strawberry Yogurt Freeze 139

Tahini 97

Tomato Salsa 69

Vegetable Dressing 85

Vegetable Soup 113

Vita Mixer 37

Whole Fruit Cherry Margarita 60

Whole Wheat Bread 129

Zucchini Pancakes 131

PASSIONATE FANS

Bright Beet Smoothie
Shared by: Donna Doyen 44

Brownie Truffles
Shared by: Sean Bowyer 151

Cashew Milk
Shared by: Brenda Crawford 64

Cherry Oatmeal Bites
Shared by: Leslie Tauro 155

Creamy Mushroom Soup
Shared by: Lance Roetling 119

Dahlia's Green Smoothie
Shared by: Heidi Barron 39

Dairy-Free Açaí Bowl
Shared by: Debra Kaplan 140

Dog Kibble Topper
Shared by: James Orth 173

Flourless Blueberry Banana Muffins
Shared by: TLP120 135

Flourless Pumpkin Muffins
Shared by: Kiran Dodeja Smith 135

Garlicky Mashed Cauliflower
Shared by: Larry L. 102

Hazelnut Spread
Shared by: Petra Scott 81

Iced Coffee Protein Drink
Shared by: Liz Enyon 63

Kale, Banana & Berry Smoothie
Shared by: Diane Mascitelli 39

Mango Nice Cream
Shared by: Tami Cockrell 140

Morning Wonder Drink
Shared by: Terry Echols 40

No-Bake Vegan Cheesecake
Shared by: Leeyel Diamond 152

Orange Sunrise Blender Drink
Shared by: Gina Fontana 48

Papaya Vanilla Smoothie
Shared by: Santiago Ortiz 40

Piña Colada Ice Cream
Shared by: Cindy Chandler 144

Plant-Based Mozzarella
Shared by: Joanne Gerrard Young 78

Protein Shake
Shared by: Debra Brock 43

Super Green Smoothie
Shared by: Cindy Molnar 51

Sweet Potato Poblano Soup
Shared by: Laine Pickrel 116

Tofu Dip
Shared by: Norma Gustafson 77

Tomato Sauce for Canning or Freezing
Shared by: Chris Applegate 98

Vegan Cheese Sauce
Shared by: Breanna Pyrda 97

Vegan Garlic Alfredo Sauce
Shared by: John Alexander McFarlane . . 101

Vegan Ricotta Cheese
Shared by: Cameron Szatala 77

VITAMIX EMPLOYEES

Ally's Asparagus Soup
Shared by: Ally Fazzalaro 125

Almond Butter Twist
Shared by: Eliot Martir 78

Beet Borani
Shared by: Karen Hicks 74

Wellness AT WORK

CORPORATE WELLNESS PROGRAM

Partnering with companies to support wellness initiatives and offer exclusive deals for employees like you.

As a Vitamix Corporate Wellness partner, your workplace can:

- SUPPORT healthy habits by offering access to a Vitamix at work.

- ENCOURAGE employee wellness at home with tips, tricks, and special promotions.

- REWARD employees by using an exclusive corporate code for awards and gifting.

For more information, contact corpwellness@vitamix.com

Berry Frozen Yogurt
Shared by: Kristie Jarrett 156

Black Bean Dip
Shared by: Laresa Waller 73

Caipirinha
Shared by: John Olsen 59

Cashew Sour Cream
Shared by: Brooke Nedrich 102

Creamy Vegan Soup Base
Shared by: Rhonda Legge 116

Frosty Strawberry Dog Treats
Shared by: Cindy Rybarczyk 170

Fruit Scrolls
Shared by: Suzanne Gagne 151

Green Lemon Sorbet
Shared by: Terrina Kramer 144

John Barnard's Green Smoothie
Shared by: John Barnard 44

Liver Treats
Shared by: Cindy Rybarczyk 170

Marinara Sauce
Shared by: Andrew Shaffer 98

Pear-Prune Purée
Shared by: Christine Carlson 165

Semisweet Green Smoothie
Shared by: Scott Tennant 48

Super Herbed Falafel
Shared by: Tamara DeGrasse 105

Super Porridge Baby Food
Shared by: Christine Carlson 162

Tomato Bell Pepper Soup
Shared by: Janae Jensen 124

Vegan Walnut & Date Pesto
Shared by: Alan Rudolph 101

VITAMIX ESSENTIALS

Almond Butter 174

Almond Milk 175

Cashew Cream 175

Coconut Milk 175

Cornmeal 177

Date Syrup 176

Oat Milk 175

Orange Juice 176

Peanut Butter 174

Peanut Cashew Butter 174

Soy Milk 176

Whole Wheat Flour 177

GRATITUDE

Most of us don't often think of our family history, but I'm privileged to live it every day. Each time I step into the Vitamix offices, I walk through our lobby and see on display the images and achievements of those who came before me and set the stage for the whole food health journey that we share today.

The small building that originally housed the Vitamix business is still a cherished part of our multi-building campus.

I'm grateful to the Vitamix employees and beloved fans around the world who shared their favorite creations, and to our talented Vitamix culinary team: Adam Wilson, Matt Dugan, and Andrew Shafer, who tested each one to ensure it meets our standards for performance, health—and most important, taste!

This cookbook was truly a multigenerational project, and I'm especially thankful for the support and encouragement from my father, John Barnard, currently our Executive Chairman. And much gratitude to my niece Robin Dieterich, who as Vitamix archivist has her finger on the vibrant pulse of our history and was a key resource for this book.

I also want to express thanks to the team, both internal and external, that collaborated to get this project across the finish line: to Adam Wilson and Scott Tennant for shepherding all the Vitamix contributors, to writer and editor Bryn Mooth for sharing her expertise, and to Brian Sooy and Vance Williams of the Aespire branding agency for guiding our self-publishing efforts, designing this cookbook, and connecting Vitamix with the people and companies in their network.

I'm so pleased that we can bring our joy and zest for life to you. **Thank you for being part of our Vitamix family.**

Jodi Berg
Jodi Berg
Vitamix President and CEO